Liberal Democracy

Liberal Democracy
A Critique of Its Theory

Andrew Levine

Columbia University Press

New York 1981

Library of Congress Cataloging in Publication Data

Levine, Andrew, 1944-
  Liberal democracy.

  Includes bibliographical references and index.
  1. Democracy. 2. Liberalism. I. Title.
JC423.L4854   321.8   81-1204
ISBN 0-231-05250-2   AACR2

Columbia University Press
New York   Guildford, Surrey

Acknowledgments

PORTIONS of chapter 2 were published in an earlier version in *Ethics* (January 1978), vol. 88, no. 2, under the title "Foundations of Unfreedom." In chapter 5, I draw on my article "A Conceptual Problem for Liberal Democracy," published in the *Journal of Philosophy* (June 1978), vol. 77, no. 6. Chapter 7 draws on my contribution to *The Philosophy of Human Rights: International Perspectives*, edited by Alan Rosenbaum, published by the Greenwood Press (1980). Chapter 10 is an expansion of my essay "The Political Theory of Social Democracy," published in the *Canadian Journal of Philosophy* (June 1976), vol. 6, no. 2. I am grateful to the editors of the three journals and the anthology for permission to make use of these materials here.

Of the many colleagues and friends whose suggestions and criticisms have found their way into these pages, I would like to thank, particularly, Mary Jo Maynes, David Resnick, Robert Paul Wolff, and Erik Olin Wright. G. A. Cohen read and commented extensively upon an earlier version of the first eight chapters. I am grateful to him for many helpful suggestions, and for saving me from some egregious errors. A special debt of gratitude is owed to my editor at Columbia University Press, Kathleen McCarthy, for her patience and support, and also for much useful advice. For financial support during the summer of 1979, when nearly all of the first draft of this book was completed, I would like to thank the Graduate School of the University of Wisconsin-Madison and the Wisconsin Alumni Research Fund.

Contents

Introduction

BY *liberal democratic theory*, I mean that genre of political theory that attempts to articulate, at the same time, both liberal and democratic judgments on political arrangements. Roughly, the liberal judgment holds that there are aspects of persons' lives, including certain kinds of activities people do, that ought to be immune from (coercive) interference by others and, above all, from state interference. The democratic judgment holds that political decisions should be determined collectively, and that collective decisions should be, at least indirectly, functions of individuals' choices among the options in contention. Political arrangements are justified, then, to the extent that they allow for the fulfillment of each of these judgments, to the extent they are both liberal and democratic.

For several centuries, the history of political theory in the West, and particularly in the English-speaking world, has been nearly coextensive with the growth, consolidation, and subsequent transformations of liberal democratic theory. Idealism, the tradition of Rousseau, Kant, Fichte, Hegel and his successors, is the only important historical rival to liberal democratic theory produced in many centuries; but even in this alternative and largely incompatible tradition, liberal democratic ideas and theoretical formulations have penetrated extensively. Arguably, Marxism poses another alternative both to idealist and liberal democratic theory. But Marxian political theory, nearly one hundred years after Marx's death, is still barely developed, even programmatically; and despite its undeniable importance as a contemporary ideology, Marxism has to date contributed very little to the political theory of the last century. Liberal democratic theory, therefore, if not quite without rivals, is today overwhelmingly dominant in political thought; and this dominance has persisted for long enough that liberal democracy may fairly be called the dominant tradition in Western political theory.

It will be objected, no doubt, that liberal democracy is mainly an affair of the nineteenth century, that the dominant tendency in political theory today, at least among writers of progressive inclinations, has to do with distributional values—with justice and perhaps even equality. Considerations of justice and equality surely are crucial, perhaps even central, in the assessment of social arrangements. For contemporary liberalism, justice may indeed be "the first virtue of social institutions."[1] And for both theoretical and practical political reasons, considerations of justice have indeed entered into contemporary political discourse and political theory. However if we focus narrowly on *political theory*, on the justifying theory of political arrangements, we find today, just as in the last century, a general unconcern for distributional values, at least in what I shall designate the *core theory* of liberal democracy. Liberal democratic theory, construed narrowly as a political theory, is generally compatible with broader liberal concerns about justice, and can accommodate such concerns in political arguments. But it is irreducible to a theory of justice. For want of a better term, let us call that type of (narrowly) political theory, commited at once to liberalism, democracy and justice (or equality), *social democratic theory*. Then my claim is that contemporary social democratic theory is, in the end, just the core theory of liberal democracy with a concern for distributional values, as it were, grafted on; that the liberal and democratic judgments on political arrangements are conceptually primary, and distributional judgments literally supplementary. However central justice or other distributional values may be for liberal social philosophy, such values are of considerably less importance in the dominant tradition's political theory than many writers today suppose.

There is plainly no reason why the judgments liberal democratic theory aims to combine should coexist easily. If the first liberals saw themselves as opponents of royal tyranny, at least so far as property and its unimpeded accumulation were threatened by the power of kings, "the tyranny of the majority" came to be seen very early on as an equal if not greater threat. The majority, as the first liberals well knew, were propertyless; and so the implementation of a program to render property holding and accumulation immune from societal and state interference seemed blatantly incompatible with the implementation of a program to make political decisions collectively. Surely the propertyless majority would exercise political power against the property-holding few. One can find a tension opposing liberalism and democracy in the writings of John Locke and his followers, in debates surrounding the American constitution, in reflections on the French Revolution and its aftermath, and even in the writings of the great consolidator of liberal democratic theory, John Stuart Mill. For liberal democrats today, this tension, like so much else the classical liberals and democrats thought problematic, is largely ignored, if even acknowledged. A theme to be investigated here is precisely the compatibility of the liberal and democratic judgments. It will be argued that liberalism and democracy cannot, after all, be combined satisfactorily, and that the liberal democratic project cannot finally succeed. Actual liberal democracy is, I will argue, a merely apparent "solution" to an insoluble problem. Its viability is to be understood historically, in view of its genesis and function, not its internal coherence or theoretical integrity.

However, difficulties in the way of constructing a political theory that is, at once, both liberal and democratic are by no means the only conceptual problems besetting liberal democracy. Each of its component "moments," the liberal and democratic strains, at least in the versions utilized in liberal democratic theoretical formulations, are, in ways not always readily apparent, themselves beset by conceptual difficulties—in their own right and, more important, in what they presuppose. The dominant tradition is so pervasive that it has become virtually "common sense." But it is nonetheless extremely problematic and vulnerable.

My account of liberal democratic theory is of necessity highly idealized, and focuses only on those features I take to be most salient. So far as possible, I have tried to reconstruct this genre of argument without extensive references to the many liberal democrats from whose writings this reconstruction is drawn. The alternative, in view of the dominance liberal democratic theory has enjoyed for so long, would be to write a history of the political theory of the past century and a half. Not only would such a project be impracticable and tedious, but a sense of perspective would surely suffer from the sheer accumulation of detail. The danger in the project undertaken here is, of course, that in abstracting from the details of actual liberal democratic positions, what is indisputably a serious body of thought may be inadvertently reduced to a caricature, against which it remains only to take cheap shots. Nonetheless, I think the task proposed here is feasible and important. Without getting to the roots of liberal democracy, considered as a genre of argument to be reconstructed, it is hardly possible to have a good sense of what the dominant tradition *is*, and to evaluate it *as such*. Such a determination is plainly useful, among other things, for the critical evaluation of particular writers and texts.

Little of interest can be said about political philosophy, as it has developed in the West, without talking also about its foundations in moral philosophy. At least since Plato, political philosophy has developed as a branch of moral philosophy, as an account of the specifically political applications of moral philosophical notions. Thus much of what follows centers on notions that are not exclusively political: on freedom,* interest, rational agency, society, human nature. I will argue that liberal democratic theory presupposes particular accounts of these notions, and that, in the senses presupposed, these notions constitute a distinct moral philosophy whose parts cohere, at least plausibly, if not always rigorously. The explication and criticism of liberal dem-

---

*Throughout what follows, "freedom" and "liberty" will be used synonymously.

ocratic theory is very largely an explication and criticism of this underlying moral philosophy.

Historically, the foundations of liberal democratic theory have been manifest, more or less explicitly, in a variety of forms: most prominently in utilitarianism, but also in social contract theories and in theories of natural rights. What distinguishes these positions is often considerable; and it will be necessary, from time to time in what follows, to explore these differences. But I will be mainly concerned with what these different moral philosophies share. It is from this common conceptual heritage that liberal democracy derives its distinctiveness, and thus its differences from the idealist tradition, from Marxism, and from earlier political philosophies.

Needless to say, the sun has not yet set on liberal democracy and thus, if Hegel is to be believed, it is too soon for philosophical investigation to proceed, too soon for the owl of Minerva to take flight. The critic of liberal democracy today does not have the advantage of retrospective hindsight, an advantage Hegel thought indispensable for providing a rational account. Against this warning, I can only agree that what follows is tentative, partial and certainly far from exhaustive. But an investigation of the sort undertaken here is anything but premature. Too much contemporary thinking about politics, particulary when attempted by philosophers in the analytic tradition, begins only after everything of importance, everything problematic, has been taken for granted. And too little attention is paid to the systematic interconnection of the issues investigated. Thus fundamental questions are ignored and the whole is obscured by even the minutest of parts. This is why, I think, analytic political philosophy, despite the best efforts of many of its practitioners, remains disappointingly superficial and irrelevant to political life. It is crucial, today above all, to look to presuppositions and to grapple with whole bodies of discourse, even if a definitive perspective remains unattainable. This task, I maintain, is feasible; even if the dangers in the way of carrying it out successfully are formidable. It is for the reader to judge how successfully these dangers have been overcome.

6 Introduction

It will be helpful at the outset to provide a brief overview of what is to follow. Part I presents a critical analysis of liberal democracy's core theory, starting from an idealized reconstruction and working back to its presuppositions. Part II examines the conceptual difficulties in the way of combining liberalism and democracy into a coherent political philosophy, and also the peculiar historical conditions that make the liberal democratic project, if not theoretically adequate, at least practically feasible. Part III, finally, examines some conceptual aspects of the historical link between liberal democracy and capitalism and speculates on the prospects for going "beyond" liberal democracy, as social democrats (in political theory) attempt, while retaining continuity with liberal democracy's core theory.

I hope to establish the following theses:

1) that liberal democratic theory presupposes a historically and conceptually distinctive framework of moral and political notions, centered around particular concepts of freedom and individual interest, and that these core concepts rest, ultimately, on a very particular—and vulnerable—notion of practical reason or (if we adopt the point of view of the agent) rational agency;

2) that liberal democratic theory, and what it presupposes, is, in a variety of ways, theoretically defective;

3) that there are (likely) insurmountable conceptual difficulties in the way of fusing liberalism and democracy together, as the liberal democractic project requires; and accordingly,

4) that it is only under the peculiar historical circumstances in which liberal democratic theory was consolidated (in the mid-nineteenth century), and under which it continues to exercise theoretical dominance, that liberal democracy, despite its theoretical shortcomings, is feasible as a political practice; and

5) that a condition for the possibility of a workable liberal

democratic politics is a very attenuated and even ambivalent commitment to democracy.

This last thesis underscores a crucial point about liberal democratic theory: that it is overwhelmingly liberal and only very tenuously democratic. Indeed, I will go on to suggest that the political institutions proper to liberal democratic polities, representative government and the party system, so far from implementing democratic values may actually betray them. Liberal democrats purport to be both liberals and democrats. Nonetheless, the political theory to which they are committed, while genuinely liberal, is not, at least in its practical implementation, genuinely democratic. I will suggest moreover that it cannot be so.

The claim that democracy and liberalism likely cannot be combined and that, under the prevailing theory and practice of politics, democracy is only apparently, but not genuinely, implemented, should not be read as a claim against what might be called *liberal values*, that is, against what liberals seek to express theoretically and to achieve practically. It is, however, a claim against theorizing liberal values, or attempting to realize them, in anything like the way historical liberalism attempts. This consideration and others of a more direct sort suggest, finally, what I take to be a principal moral of this study and a central theme of its concluding section:

> 6) that those who are committed to democracy and also to liberal values (as distinct from liberal theoretical formulations and liberal political institutions) should seek to develop a different, and more adequate, theory and practice of politics.

My quarrel, again, is not with liberal democratic, and still less with social democratic, intentions, at least if these intentions are construed generally enough to avoid commitment to the peculiar constellation of concepts and institutions liberal and social democrats characteristically endorse. My quarrel instead is with the dominant tradition's theoretical expression of these intentions and, above all, with the politics that, we shall see, motivates this theoretical stance.

I do not mean to deny that there is much of value in the liberal democratic tradition. Liberal democratic polities are, by virtually any standard, improvements over the forms of political association they came to supplant, and arguably also over other contemporary forms of social and political organization. But this sort of comparative assessment pales before the overwhelming shortcomings of liberal democratic politics, above all in the present historical conjuncture. One need only look about unblinded to see that citizens of liberal democratic states are deprived of most of the foreseeable benefits of genuinely democratic political experience, and even of many of the advantages of liberty. More pressing still, liberal democracies, again today as in the past, pose increasingly grave hazards for international peace and order; and even if their political forms do not account for this menace, neither do they impede its onset and development. To be sure, many within the liberal democratic camp are aware of these and other shortcomings, and have set about to develop remedies. But, if I am right, either these remedies will be of no avail or else their connection to liberal democratic theory will be so tenuous as to belie any pretense of continuity. Then, whatever its merits, it is politically urgent that an alternative to liberal democracy be developed and constructed. Admittedly, the dominant theory and practice of politics has not been an unmitigated evil—indeed, quite the contrary. But it is nonetheless an evil that the world today could well do without.

This essay, then, is an attack on a still reigning ancien regime, in the guise of a critique of its theory. It would be desirable, of course, to be able to propose a positive alternative to liberal democracy, an outline of a different—and better—theory and practice of politics. But to attempt anything so ambitious and speculative, in the absence of developed alternatives, would be useless and foolhardy. Even if philosophers need not, indeed must not, wait for the setting of the sun, as Hegel insisted, they can hardly command a new sun to rise. It seemed a decade ago that a mounting struggle in all the advanced capitalist countries against the existing, liberal democratic order might indeed engender a new politics, whether in the form of a revived Marxism or on the basis of even less developed political theories. As the 1980's begin, needless to say, these prospects seem distant. The dominant tradition appears secure, even as the politics it justifies mounts disaster after disaster. But this security is false. The continuing ancien regime under which we live is vulnerable, and while it is far from assured that we would be better off for the demise of liberal democracy, we can at least begin to see, even now, that a genuinely democratic politics, however difficult to achieve and even to theorize, is possible and therefore necessary.

Part I / The Core Theory and Its Foundations

AN important contribution of Kant's to philosophical method is the defense and elaboration of what he calls "regressive analysis," according to which the philosopher investigates certain propositions, the truth and necessity of which are generally admitted (the propositions of geometry, the claims of morality) and argues back to the existence of certain conditions without which they could not have the truth and necessity which in fact they have. I would not wish to claim that there are any true and necessary propositions definitive of liberal democratic theory, but there are, I think, distinctive theoretical positions that do, in turn, have distinctive conditions for their possibility. My intent in Part I is to explore these distinctive positions and to bring their presuppositions to light. Thus Part I attempts something like a regressive analysis of liberal democratic theory: starting from an idealized reconstruction of this genre of argument (chapter 1), working back through its presupposed notions of freedom (chapter 2) and interest (chapter 3), culminating in an account of practical reason or rational agency (chapter 4).

Since the overall purview of this study is critical, I focus on points of vulnerability. And to draw liberal democratic theory into sharper focus, I somethimes contrast its positions with those of its principal rival, idealism, and also with other traditions of political thought. These comparisons are often to liberal democratic theory's detriment. Even so, my intent throughout Part I is more expository than expressly critical. There is a case against liberal democratic theory, and what it presupposes, that can be gleaned from these four chapters; but their chief role, in the general scheme of this book, is as prolegomenon to the more directly critical forays launched in Parts II and III.

Liberal democratic theory has had so many different incarnations over the decades it has dominated political thought that an idealized reconstruction, no matter how abstracted from actual political discourse, is bound to be partial and idiosyncratic. Undoubtedly, others would focus on different aspects, or would construe those liberal democratic positions I do discuss differently. It is not at all my intention to present the definitive account of liberal democratic theory, but only to get a purchase on it sufficient for investigating the (theoretical) conditions for its possibility. Even so, the risk of caricaturing an extensive and complex tradition is considerable. I can only reiterate my conviction that a regressive analysis of liberal democratic theory is feasible, and that the benefits of undertaking so perilous a project vastly outweigh the hazards.

1 / An Overview
of Liberal Democratic Theory

A neglect of fundamental questions has always characterized liberal democratic writings. The great themes of seventeenth- and
eighteenth-century political philosophy, and their continuations
in more recent idealist thought—the problems of authority, sovereignty and political obligation—are seldom directly treated
throughout the entire, massive corpus of liberal democratic literature. Instead, what seventeenth and eighteenth-century democratic theorists regarded as a lesser question, concerning the *limits* rather than the nature of political authority, effectively supercedes
all others. What are the proper limits, if any, of the state's (and,
more generally, society's) right to interfere (coercively) with individuals' lives? This is the question addressed directly by John
Stuart Mill in *On Liberty*, the *locus classicus* along with *Considerations on Representative Government*, of liberal democratic theory. Many contemporary liberal democrats do not even think to
address this question, though they assume positions with respect
to it. But even if unaddressed, for liberal democrats, this question
becomes, in effect, the fundamental question of political life.

A theory of the (legitimate) limits of state power is of course
not specific to liberal democratic theory. Such a theory is propsed,
for example, by Rousseau in chapters 4 and 5 of Book II of *The
Social Contract*. But Rousseau's position follows directly from an
explicit account of the nature of sovereignty. For Mill, in contrast,
the question of limits stands on its own. That question becomes

the fundamental theoretical question, as it were, by default—because it is, in effect, the only question asked.

Indeed, it is astonishing that for all its dominance of political thought, there exists no full-scale, liberal democratic justifying theory of political institutions.[1] Thus to assert, as I have, that, for liberal democrats, political institutions are justified to the extent that liberal and democratic values are realized by these institutions is already to cast liberal democratic theory in a form it implicitly rejects, the form of grand political philosophy. However this rejection of justification on the grand scale, though hardly accidental, is not principled or theoretically well-motivated. Liberal democratic theory can be reconstructed as a justifying theory of the traditional type; and it is in that form that it will be considered here.

Doubtless the change in focus from the grand political theories of Hobbes and Locke to the more restricted and superficial concerns of liberal democrats are largely the result of specific, historical transformations. The social and political reorganization of seventeenth- and eighteenth-century Europe—the dissolution of feudal society, the emergence of the nation state and the first intimations of popular power—all cast traditional notions of authority and obligation into crisis. The old, inherited assumptions proved inadequate to the new social experience. Political life had to be rethought, its foundations reconstructed and its fundamental assumptions transformed. By the early and mid-nineteenth century, however, the time of the consolidation of liberal democratic theory by Mill and others, this crisis was effectively resolved—not, to be sure, by the elaboration of an adequate theory of the just state, but by a *fait accompli*, the irreversible consolidation of existing states. The problems grand political philosophy investigated were hardly settled, but they were no longer quite so pressing as they had seemed.

Other problems had come to the fore. With the dissolution of feudal society and the resulting atomization of social relations, the problem of the *individual* and his *rights* was posed for the first time (if exception is made of some superficially similar questions asked by Aristotle and other political thinkers of the ancient world). And with the full development of the nation state and the progressive extension of the democratic franchise, extensive political interference, as opposed to restrictions of tradition, custom or opinion, became a live possibility. The question liberal democratic theory focuses upon, then, is hardly an eternal question, but a very particular one historically, posed, in effect, by the social experience of triumphant capitalism and the emergence of the system of nation-states. Liberal democratic theory, in short, responds to a later moment of Western political experience than its bolder and more radical forebearers. It is the theory of an established, not an emergent, order. Its conceptual problems are those generated, so to speak, *within* that order, rather than *between* that order and its historical rivals.

It is not surprising, then, when liberal democratic theory is reconstructed as a full-fledged justifying theory, to find that it turns out to depend substantially on its predecessors. To address their central concerns, liberal democrats are, needless to say, selective (implicitly) in their use of the past; and, on occasion, liberal democrats find it necessary, in effect, to modify inherited positions. But even so, there is remarkably little *new*, with respect to either liberalism or democracy, that can be ascribed to liberal democracy. Liberal democratic theory is much more an amalgam of ideas, a fusion of positions, than a new synthesis.

What is novel in liberal democratic theory is just the attempt to combine liberal and democratic positions, each already developed separately—and sometimes even antagonistically—into a unified theory. In the proposed unification, the liberal and democratic strains remain virtually intact. For that reason, we can consider these strains, at least initially, in relative isolation from one another.

The democratic strain, though less prominent in the liberal democratic literature, and *much less important* (as we shall go on to see) in liberal democratic politics, is, from the point of view of grand political theory, the more fundamental. It supplies the liberal democratic account of the nature of political authority and obligation. The liberal strain, centering on the question of political authority's limits, is, however, the practicing liberal democrat's major preoccupation. It supplies the tone and character of liberal democratic theory. It will be well, then, to turn first to the liberal component of the liberal democratic fusion.

The Liberal Strain

In the first instance, what distinguishes liberalism from other political positions is its insistence on specifying determinate limits to political authority. This stance, I would suggest, is a consequence of a profound distrust and even hostility towards politics that must be grasped, if liberalism, as the most distinctive component of the dominant political theory, is to be properly understood and appreciated.

In opposition to Rousseau and also to Aristotle and much of the classical tradition, liberalism supposes a singular and radical separation of the political from the social, of politics from society.[2] Today the concepts of a non-political "civil society" and of politics, existing, so to speak, outside society, apart from ordinary social life, have become so deeply entrenched, so much a part of the common sense view of the world, that it requires sustained intellectual effort even to conceive society interpenetrated and structured by politics, as it is in the ideal theory of *The Social Contract*. We are accustomed to regard politics apart from society and subordinated to it. For better or worse, we assume, as did Locke, that the social order engenders and supports political arrangements, and not, as Rousseau contended, the reverse.

No doubt the pervasiveness of this assumption is, at least partly, a consequence of liberal democracy's long dominance. But it is compatible with many non-liberal theoretical positions as well. The structural subordination of politics to society is characteristic of some idealist political philosophy, particularly after Hegel, and, though with greater complexity than is usually assumed, also of Marxism. What is distinctive about liberalism, among modern political theories, is the radical devaluation of politics that follows from its separation from and subordination to society. Society is where what is essentially human is played out. It is the sphere of freedom and (practical) reason. If, as we shall see, politics is unavoidable, necessitated by the human condition itself, its proper function, for liberals, is just the maintenance of society, of the sphere of apolitical, individual activity. At best, the state is a neutral means for maintaining this sphere; more often, it is regarded as a necessary evil. Political institutions, are not valued for their own sake, but for the prevention of even greater misfortune.

Historically, then, liberalism affiliates, as did Hobbes, with the anti-classical, Augustinian tradition in Western political thought: the tradition that denies positive value to political life and depicts the state as an artifice concocted to save humanity from itself. For St. Augustine, this unhappy conclusion follows from a systematic, theological view of history in which politics is one of the odious condemnations of Fallen Man, through which Providence, in ways generally inscrutable, works its designs. For secularists like Hobbes, it is human psychology that motivates a similar view of politics. Individuals are such that if left to pursue their own ends, without coercive control, a "war of all against all" would follow, rendering life "solitary, poor, nasty, brutish and short," and generally impeding the realization of the very ends, the pursuit of which engenders a state of war. Politics, then, is a concession to the human-all-too-human. it is not an end in itself, but a means for allowing persons' ends, however conceived, to be fulfilled elsewhere and in other ways. (For Hobbes, these ends nonetheless remain shaped by the fact of political association. For Augustine, so depraved is humanity in consequence of Original Sin, that each person's true end, incorporation in the City of God, cannot be achieved through "works" of any sort, buy only through unmerited grace, and, even so, only at the Final Judgment).

Liberalism differs from its predecessors in the Augustinian tradition just in its insistence on the separation of politics from society (unlike Hobbes), and in its easy optimism, according to which the realization of worthwhile ends—in *society*—is relatively unproblematic (unlike Augustine). This is not to say that, for liberals, society is valued for its own sake, that "association" or "community" are values. Indeed, for the early liberals, at least, very nearly the opposite is the case. Rather, it is in society—that is, *not* in the state—that individuals' ends are realizable. As we shall see, this characteristic position is a consequence of the notion of freedom liberalism presupposes. If society, not the state, is the realm of self-fulfillment or self-realization, it is because society, not the state, is the realm of freedom.

For idealists such as Rousseau or Kant, freedom is understood as *autonomy*, as rational self-determination. One is free to the degree that (practical) reason is in control, unfree—heteronomously determined—otherwise. Thus one is unfree, in Kant's view, even when one obeys no other individual's will, but only one's own inclinations or one's own calculations of self-interest. For liberals, in contrast, there is no sense of freedom having to do with rational self-determination. And neither is there any point in talking about freedom (or the absence of freedom) in general. One is free (or unfree) to do something (or to refrain from doing something). Freedom is not so much a state of being, as it is for the idealists, as a relation between persons and acts. Moreover, in the liberal view, freedom is a social relation, a relation between persons. One is free (or unfree) to do (or refrain from doing) some act *with respect to others*. Roughly, then, freedom for liberalism is the absence of coercive restraint or interference.* Freedom is emphatically not autonomy in the Rousseauean or Kantian sense, but only, if liberals talk of "autonomy" at all, in the ordinary sense of "independence," of the absence of interference by others. The notion of rational self-determination, as we shall go on to see, is virtually unintelligible for liberals. On the other hand, the presence (or absence) of coercive interference matters little, if at all,

---

*For the present, it will suffice to use terms such as "coercive restraint," "coercive interference," "the use of threat of force," etc. interchangeably. For purposes of more careful analysis, it may be necessary to establish finer distinctions, however.

for idealists. One can even be "forced to be free," as Rousseau declares paradoxically but in earnest in *The Social Contract*; one can be made free by being forced to do what reason requires and therefore what one *really* wants as a rational agent. For the liberal, though, one can never be forced to be free. To be forced is *ipso facto* to be unfree.

Thus, for liberals, the use or threat of force always restricts freedom. In society, behavior is generally not coordinated by the use or threat of force and is, therefore, free. The state, however, is a coercive institution. "Like the political institutions historically preceding it," Max Weber wrote, "the state is a relation of men dominating men, a relation supported by means of legitimate (i.e., considered to be legitimate) violence."[3] Needless to say, the state is not only coercive. Indeed, no state could exist for very long just by the use of threat of force. In any well-functioning polity, consensus largely replaces explicit coercion. This is the sense of Hume's well-known remark that "it is on opinion only . . . that government is founded." Force is the basis upon which the state rests, but for actually coordinating behavior, "opinion" plays the dominant role. Thus it is only in the last resort, when consensus breaks down, that the real foundation of the state, its foundation in violence, reveals itself for all to see. But even so, in its ordinary operations, with "opinion" soundly in place, the state coordinates behavior coercively. It speaks to the citizen in laws that impose sanctions for failure to comply. To this extent, then, even in its day by day functioning, the state renders persons unfree. It works by restricting freedom.

Thus liberalism reverses the idealist insistence that freedom is realized only in the state. For Rousseau, the just state is the condition for the possibility of autonomous self-determination. For Hegel, the state is, as he would have it, "the realization of the idea of Freedom." But for the liberal, the state is the realm of unfreedom. So far as the state acts to coordinate behavior, with respect to the state, its subjects are unfree.

Is the liberal, then, at least tendentially an anarchist, an opponent of states? One might suppose so, given the liberal's commitment to freedom. But even so, liberals plainly are not anarchists. However inimical to freedom, liberalism regards the state as necessary. For by restricting freedom, the state supports freedom. It allows for the realization of freedom *elsewhere*, apart from the state, in society.

Seventeenth- and eighteenth-century forebears of liberalism vigilantly maintained the need for states, even as they valued freedom. Thus Hobbes argued that the freedom of the state of nature, unrestricted by any public coercive force, is self-defeating, and, in effect, requires the institution of sovereignty for its full realization. The argument is well known and can be recounted briefly. Since people coexist in the same geographical territory making conflicting demands on the same scarce resources, and since they are sufficiently equal in mental and physical endowments to be able to harm one another, individually or collectively, and since they are psychologically inclined to seek to accumulate resources virtually without limit, people find themselves continually in mortal competition with everyone for everything. In this "state of war," individuals' ends are generally unrealizable, and thus their freedom, Hobbes insisted, is in vain. But these same people find they are able, at least sometimes, to make themselves better off by cooperating with one another. Thus a framework for regulating conflict and facilitating cooperation comes to be in each person's interest as a free agent. But such a framework is incompatible with the state of nature. For in the absence of a public coercive force, a sovereign, each person, whatever his stake in the maintenance of civil order, has an incentive, given his interests, not to abide by the agreements that would insure this order. Thus if the state of war is to be avoided, as all parties want, there must be an enforcer whose function, in effect, is to guarantee conformity to the agreements that are in each party's interest. On Hobbes' account, all individuals "authorize" such an enforcer—as much to restrain themselves as to restrain others—and thereby definitively end the state of war. The point is to raise the cost of disobedience to a level where general compliance becomes the interest of each party. Thus, for Hobbes, the "absolute freedom" of the state of nature paradoxically diminishes freedom, and is therefore contrary to our interests as free, rational beings, seeking to realize our ends without restraint. It is in each person's interest, accordingly, to move away from absolute freedom by establishing a state. Some freedom is sacrificed in order that freedom may be realized, to the extent human nature and the human situation allow. The state is the price we pay, in other words, for achieving that degree of freedom that is *optimal*, given our situation and our interests as free beings.

Hobbes, of course, believed that the state is possible only if its power is in principle unlimited; and on this count, the liberal cannot follow. But whatever differences there may be between liberals and Hobbes on this central question of liberal political philosophy, the liberal's rationale for establishing sovereignty (that is, limited sovereignty), to the extent a rationale can be provided, is basically the same as Hobbes'. For both Hobbes and the liberals, the state, in coordinating behavior coercively, detracts from freedom. But the absence of a state is a far more devastating blow for freedom. It is in our interests, then, as free beings to submit to the rigors of political life. In doing so, we give up something in order to save much more.

Were freedom the only value political institutions seek to protect, it would follow, as it has for many liberals, that the best political arrangements would be minimal ones: leaving each individual free, so far as possible, to pursue his ends in society. The good state will interfere no more than is necessary to insure that the optimal level of freedom is realized. Thus it is sometimes held that the state or, more exactly, its institutional embodiment, the government, ought to be no more than society's "nightwatchman," insuring just that the rules for regulating competition and organizing cooperation are adhered to, and perhaps also its "referee," resolving disputes wherever they arise. The nightwatchman, the referee, is unfortunately indispensable, but the government that governs if not least, as some would have it, but rather as little as strictly necessary, governs best.*

Thus to suppose a strict separation of politics from society, a subordination of the former to the latter, and also to value freedom in the liberals' sense, is to generate a powerful presumption for contracting politics, for minimizing the role of governments, and for expanding society, the sphere of individual, apolitical activity. Constrained only so much as to avoid "the war of all against all," the individual should be left free from coercive control. Since this presumption, however powerful, is not yet a full-fledged principle, marking off an area of non-interference, it is, strictly speaking, compatible with any content. For this reason, I shall call a political theory where this liberal presumption figures importantly, *formal liberalism*. For formal liberalism, any interference *may* be legitimate, but the burden of proof is always on whoever would propose the interference. Formal liberalism need not, strictly, entail a minimal state and a nightwatchman or referee theory of government, just because there might be admissible grounds for coercive interference with others' behavior that have nothing to do with insuring that the optimal level of freedom is realized. For example, a formal liberal might regard the promotion of social welfare or even the enforcement of morality as legitimate grounds for interfering coercively with others' behavior. Then the state might legitimately do a good deal more than what partisans of a minimal state would maintain. But even so, liberals are always committed to maximizing freedom, whatever else they may be committed to as well; and thus they are always, at least tenden-

---

*The case for the minimal state is also sometimes made by appeal to welfare considerations, at least by defenders of "free markets." Roughly the argument could be made as follows: if free markets promote social welfare (as defenders of markets widely insist), then any state interference with the market mechanism can only diminish aggregate welfare. Thus to promote welfare, it is necessary to restrict states at least to the point where they do not interfere with the workings of the market mechanism. The premise of this argument, however, that free markets promote social welfare, is plausible only on very unrealistic assumptions about how markets work, and so this sort of case for the minimal state is seldom heard today.

tially, partisans of the minimal state, even if this tendency may be, and often is, countervailed.

Formal liberalism is a regulative ideal. According to that ideal, governmental or other coercive interference is an evil to be avoided, other things being equal. But formal liberalism provides no indication as to when other things are equal, and as such it fails to rule out any particular interferences. Formal liberalism, in short, is purely formal. This is why, characteristically, liberal writers, at least during liberalism's "golden age," sought to give this regulative ideal substantive content, to mark off an area in which interference is deemed illegitimate. Mill's attempt to distinguish a "private sphere" of self-regarding actions and experiences of private consciousness from a "public sphere" of other-regarding actions is exemplary. So too was Locke's attempt, revived recently in some quarters,[4] to specify inviolable individual rights. The presumption is always for non-interference. But interference is in principle permissible in some cases, and categorically excluded in others. A position of this sort, that adds to formal liberalism some concrete specification of an area of non-interference, thereby giving substantive content to liberalism's regulative ideal, I shall call *substantive liberalism*. The kinds of liberal arguments that constitute liberal democratic theory cluster around the substantive pole, even if, for reasons to be explored below in Part II, an adequate substantive theory remains elusive.

In sum, then, it is a commitment to a certain view of freedom and also to a certain view of politics and its relation to society that motivate both formal and substantive liberalism. It is perhaps already sufficiently clear how particular these views are. This particularity will be a central issue in what follows. In any case, the democratic component, as we shall now go on to see, rests on different, but not unrelated, commitments.

The Democratic Strain

Just as a special, historically particular concept of freedom underlies and motivates the liberal component of liberal democratic theory, an equally special and historically particular concept of individual *interest* underlies and motivates the democratic component. The term "interest" in fact functions in many very different ways in contemporary political discourse. Here I shall focus only on that sense of the term according to which, in the final analysis, a person's wants or desires (I shall use these terms interchangeably) determine his interests. I will therefore not address notions of "interest" that make essential reference to human needs, except insofar as wants and needs coincide, nor shall I be concerned with "interest" as an ideal or standard of what is good for a person, independent of his wants. I am skeptical whether these and other senses of "interest," whatever their role in contemporary political discussions, can in fact be properly accommodated within a liberal democratic conceptual framework, but it is not my intention to explore this question here. My concern, instead, is just with that sense of "interest" that motivates the liberal democrat's commitment to democracy.

To be sure, liberal democratic theory assumes no simple identity of wants and interests. Interests may deviate from express wants or even oppose them. But, ultimately, even where wants and interests conflict, interest, in the sense in question, is founded upon desire. A person's interests, then, are as uniquely his own as are his wants. This is why no trans-individual, ideal standard that abstracts from persons' wants—even if only to specify "true needs" or "rational desires"—can ever justify the ascription of interests to persons. In a word, desire is the *source* of interest.

We shall see in chapter 4 that this sense of "interest" rests on a distinctive understanding of rationality, according to which practical reason is purely instrumental, concerning the adapting of means to ends, but not the content of the ends themselves. For liberal democrats, as for adherents of related social philosophies, reason is, as Hume declared, "the slave of the passions."[5] Or, as Jeremy Bentham would have it: "it is by hopes and fears that the ends of actions are determined; all reason does is to find and determine the means."[6]

Were there always means at our disposal adequate for realizing the ends of actions, the ideally rational person would be the perfectly efficient person, the person who realizes his ends (acts in his own interest) most economically. However success in realizing our ends cannot be taken as the measure of rationality. Efficiency is always relative to the parameters imposed by the situation, and our world, unfortunately, is not sufficiently abundant to secure us all the ends we seek, particularly when other persons, with other ends, make conflicting demands on the same scarce resources. Some of our ends, moreover, are simply unrealizable, given available resources; and for others, such as happiness, no means can ever in principle be complete. The rational agent, then, is the one who does the best he can, given his ends, and given his situation. Rational activity is maximizing activity. It is not efficiency in realizing ends, but efficiency in pursuing them.[7]

Where practical reason is understood this way, we may suppose that a person's ends, however diverse and apparently incommensurable, can be ranked on a single, quantitative scale, according to his degree of preference for their realization. This quantitative measure of preference is *utility*. Thus we can say that to be rational is to be a utility maximizer.

We have just seen that absolute freedom, the freedom of the state of nature, is self-defeating and therefore contrary to our interests as free beings. But absolute freedom is just unlimited freedom to maximize utility. Thus the Hobbesian argument for the state, sketched above, can be restated, more perspicuously and with important additional implications, in terms of our interests as utility maximizers. Unlimited freedom to maximize utility, given Hobbesian assumptions about human nature, given circumstances of relative scarcity, and given finally the fact that human beings are relatively equal in nature and therefore mutually vulnerable, results in a "war of all against all" in which persons do less well for themselves as utility maximizers than they otherwise might. Accordingly, arrangements for regulating conflict and organizing cooperation are in each person's interest. But where such arrangements are instituted, there remains, as we have seen, a literal and potentially devastating conflict of interest. For individuals will also have interests, very often, in disobeying whatever rules are established, so long as this act of disobedience does not, on balance, have untoward consequences. Thus if there are rules against stealing money, a utility maximizer with continuous positive utility for money, will have *both* an interest in general conformity to the rule (and therfore in obeying the rule himself) and also in individually violating the rule, whenever it is advantageous for him to do so.*Moreover, in these circumstances, it is likely that lone disobedience will be preferred to individual conformity; so it is likely that a mutually advantageous framework for regulating competition and organizing cooperation, even when in the interest of everyone, will break down. Thus agreement alone is insufficient for ending the state of nature. We must also tie our hands in such a way that the rules we agree to will prevail, despite the continuing interests of each of us in acting contrary to our agreements. The problem, in short, is to insure conformity to rules. Hobbes' solution is to establish sovereignty. Thus the sovereign is instituted, in Hobbes' view, to complete what agreement alone cannot achieve. And as we have seen, liberal democracy implicitly takes over this rationale.

However the liberal democrat, for whom individuals' interests ultimately reduce to individuals' wants, is not content to stop where Hobbes stopped. The Hobbesian sovereign, once established, acts without further regard for individuals' interests. It is simply enough that the sovereign exists. It is as though all systems of rules, in Hobbes' view, are of equal merit, and the enforcement

---

*One negative consequence of lone disobedience, for those who have an interest in general conformity to the rule, is that one's *own* disobedience may undermine the tendency of others to conform to the rule. Presumably, utility maximizers will consider such consequences in calculating whether or not to disobey. This sort of consideration should not be confused, however, with the sort of *universalization* argument that has figured in philosophical reflections on moral rules throughout the history of Western political philosophy. In universalization arguments, the point is to abstract from what distinguishes oneself as an individual from other individuals; to consider one's interest as a *pure* moral agent, without idiosyncratic desires and aversions. On the other hand, the calculation supposed here depends crucially on one's concrete individuality. It is our desires and aversions that determine whether, in any particular case, conformity or nonconformity is in our interest.

of any system equally desireable. But the liberal democrat supposes, very plausibly, that some forms of authority are preferable to others, that some are better than others in accommodating individuals' interests. For the democrat, concern for realizing individuals' interests requires not only that there be states, but also that states function so as to accord best with these interests, as they exist and change over time. The liberal democrat therefore *corrects* Hobbes, calling for not just any sovereign, but for a sovereign continually responsive to individuals' interests.

These interests must, then, be expressed and combined; and the results should determine what the sovereign does. What is required, in short, is a collective decision procedure for combining expressions of individuals' interests to produce social choices in accord with these interests. This collective decision procedure in effect replaces the Hobbesian sovereign. Thus the argument *for* the state that liberal democrats (implicitly) take over from Hobbes is extended to account for the form and nature of the state.

Note that for the liberal democrat, unlike the plain liberal, the realization of the optimal level of freedom is not the sole rationale for states and is likewise not the sole evaluative principle proper for assessing political arrangements. In addition to considerations of freedom, an aggregative concern—that political association should maximize the amount of interest (i.e., want-) satisfaction among individuals in a political community—also figures in assessments. If the liberal values freedom alone, the liberal democrat values (at least) freedom and welfare. Doubtless many political disputes among liberal democrats depend, to some extent at least, on the relative weights assigned to these different concerns.*

---

*It is worth noting that in *On Liberty*, Mill purports to provide utilitarian justifications for liberal freedoms. Mill must believe, then, that rather than freedom and welfare conflicting, freedom always promotes welfare. The fact that other liberal democrats do see conflicts, and disagree accordingly with many of Mill's express views on the proper role of the state, indicates that Mill's view of the relation between freedom and welfare is overly optimistic. But we should resist the temptation to go to the other extreme, maintaining that freedom and welfare are antagonistic values, and that the task of sound public policy is to discover the best "trade'offs" between them.

Note too that whatever the liberal democrat's debt to Hobbes, this view of the nature and proper functioning of the sovereign entails far-reaching changes in Hobbes' account of sovereignty. Hobbes' sovereign is not a party to "the social contract" that, in Hobbes' view, institutes sovereignty. For Hobbes, individuals contract among themselves to transfer or alienate all rights of self-determination to a third party that remains outside the social contract and agrees to nothing. Thus the Hobbesian sovereign, this third party, receives, as it were, a donation of power for which he is not, strictly speaking, accountable. In disputing this conclusion, so far as the concern is to further individuals' interests, the liberal democrat, in effect, shifts the sceptre of sovereignty away from any third party, apart from the people, to the people themselves. In this way, liberal democracy commits itself to a notion of popular sovereignty.

The position just sketched differs substantially from justifications for popular sovereignty and democratic collective decision procedures found elsewhere—in the idealist wing of the classical democratic tradition. Thus for Rousseau, far from furthering individuals' ("private") interests, popular sovereignty is held to be incompatible with such interests. For Rousseau, the just state requires the "supercession" (and also the suppression) of what the liberal democrat seeks to advance, the private interests of individuals. Voting, for Rousseau, is therefore not a mechanism for aggregating private interests, for discovering what Rousseau pejoratively calls "the will of all." Instead it is viewed as a procedure for discovering the "general interest" which, for each voter, supercedes private interest in the just state.[8] Both Rousseau and the liberal democrat are democrats: each is committed to collective decision procedures that generate social choices out of individual choices. And each subscribes to a notion of popular sovereignty. But what underlies and motivates these positions is entirely different.

We have seen that a commitment to democratic collective choice leads liberal democrats to a theory of popular sovereignty. We should realize, however, that these commitments *can* diverge.

It might be thought, for example, that the sovereign people form an entity that is somehow independent of the particular individuals who constitute it, so that these individuals' choices need not figure at all in the determination of the sovereign people's choices. Or it might be held that there is a dependence of some sort between the sovereign people and the people who collectively constitute the sovereign, but that one can abstract from it, for purposes of deciding upon public policy, and proceed *as if* the people had a personality and will of its own, somehow ascertainable independently of collective decision procedures. Some idealist political philosophy, particularly in versions influenced by Hegel, seems to subscribe to one or another of these views. But in doing so, whatever its continuing commitment to popular sovereignty, idealism parts ways with the democratic tradition. Where the people are sovereign, it is natural to suppose that what the sovereign does should be a function of what all and only the sovereign people want it to do, and that the people should express their collective will by combining their individual choices. If popular sovereignty does not strictly entail democratic collective choice, it certainly suggests it.

The collective decision procedures of greatest interest to democrats are, of course, voting procedures. For the liberal democrat, who seeks to accommodate individuals' interests best in order to attain the aggregative maximum, it is reasonable, moreover, to opt for voting procedures that respond most directly to voters' choices. It is for this reason that majority rule voting is particularly attractive.

One might think that if a collective choice is to promote individuals' interest that it should be able to secure unanimous approval. Might we not, then, as an alternative to majority rule voting, require unanimity? This is indeed what some defenders of "free markets" maintain. Market allocations are unanimously chosen in the sense that they result, by definition, from bilateral voluntary exchanges. Therefore, it is maintained, everyone freely chooses the outcome. We shall examine this very dubious claim in chapter 9. For now, it should be clear that, at least as a voting procedure, unanimity is hardly responsive to voters' choices. When unanimity is not achieved, no change away from the status quo can be realized. Each voter has effective veto power. Thus if the status quo is *y* and 99 out of 100 voters prefer *x* to *y*, *y* remains the collective choice. The same difficulty holds in diminishing degree as we approach simple majority rule for any majority rule voting system requiring more than a simple numerical majority to make a positive enactment. Thus the procedure most responsive to individuals' interests and therefore most consonant with democratic intuitions is simple majority rule voting.

The presumption in favor of majority rule voting will often be countered by a conservative inclination to bias collective choice in favor of the status quo. The intuition is that wisdom dictates caution, that the status quo is at least workable, and that change is risky (and seldom worth the risk). We ought, then, to bias our decision procedures against change—except of course where there is overwhelming desire for it (as expressed in appropriately large majorities). The more fundamental the measure in question, the more compelling conservative caution seems. With basic changes, the danger of going disastrously wrong is far greater than with lesser proposals for change. No doubt this is why democratic theorists of all tendencies often argue for large majorities (and sometimes other safeguards as well) for important measures, and particularly for measures bearing on "constitutional" questions. There is, no doubt, considerable wisdom in such caution. But this wisdom is not, strictly speaking, part of liberal democracy's core theory. It is a *corrective,* an outside consideration, in the sense that for Aristotle in the *Nicomachean Ethics,* considerations of "equity" mitigate and thereby correct the requirements of strict, distributive justice. Liberal democrats may often, in varying degrees, show conservative inclinations and thus shy away from majoritarianism; but liberal democracy in itself tends towards majoritarianism.

In producing the most preferred outcome, majority rule voting also produces the *fairest* outcome. If all existing interests are expressed, as they must be if everyone votes, the outcome reflects the relative strengths of the different interests expressed. In this sense, majority rule voting is just; and deviations from majority rule voting, even if warranted for conservative or other reasons, are deviations from strict justice.

The justice in question is, however, justice in voting procedures. Liberal democratic theory, as reconstructed here, takes no direct concern with patterns of distribution. Its commitment to majority rule follows from an aggregative, not a distributional consideration. The point is to maximize welfare, not to realize desirable distributions of benefits and burdens. Justice in the sense of fairness figures at all only because to promote welfare successfully, individuals' interests must be handled fairly.

It should be noted, finally, that the case for the democratic component suggests, ideally, that social choices be made directly rather than through the mediation of representatives. Yet liberal democratic politics, without exception, rely on representative institutions of one sort or another. In functioning liberal democracies, if not in the core theory of liberal democracy, the people do not legislate directly, but through representative legislators, vested with considerable power to determine social choices, sometimes even in complete independence of the views, express or implicit, of the people they represent. We shall return to the question of representative government in chapter 8. We shall see that there is a deep tension, if not an outright contradiction, between the theoretical commitments of the core theory and its implementation in representative institutions; but that, at the same time, representative government is the sole practical "solution" to the problem of joining liberalism and democracy.

There is a tension too between liberal democracy's aggregative concerns and its view of politics and society. If the state is only a necessary evil, why expect it to further individuals' interests? It is perhaps a sense of this tension that accounts, at least in part, for the thoroughgoing subordination of democracy to liberalism that pervades so much liberal democratic theory and practice. In acceding to the need for states, liberal democracy, as it were, latches onto an aggregative value, to make a virtue of necessity. But the tension remains. In this sense, Hobbes is more consistent than the liberal democrat. If states are necessary evils, then evils they must be. It is a shallow palliative to seek to build in aggregative virtues.

Even the method of majority rule cannot undo the state's role as a source, indeed the principal source, of unfreedom. Where the majority determines the minority, those in the minority are forced to do what they do not want to do and are therefore unfree. Rousseau and other idealists could avoid this result by supposing that there is a general interest (for all voters) that the majority discovers. Then in being compelled by the majority, individuals in the minority are compelled to do what they really want (though they didn't know it), and are thus "forced to be free." But if, as for liberal democratic theory, there are only independent individual interests, private interests in Rousseau's sense, and no general interest to be discovered, the idealist way out is unavailable. Then the price of even the most responsive and fairest collective decision procedure is some restriction on liberty. Even where, to the greatest extent possible, political institutions further individuals' interests, they are not, even for those individuals, an unmixed blessing, but rather a way of cutting losses in a world where the state of nature, a condition of absolute freedom, is sadly untenable.

2 / Freedom

THE characteristic eclecticism and imprecision of political discourse, and of philosophical thought about politics, is nowhere more striking than in talk of *freedom*. For its entire recent history, freedom has been central to Western political practice and its theory. Revolutions have been made for freedom; systems of government and even forms of the state have been overthrown and reconstructed for the sake of this ideal. Like justice, freedom has been conflated with virtually all political and moral values, no matter how diverse. And residues of the most distant political philosophies continue to survive in contemporary uses of the term. Even in orthodox, liberal writings, the term is encumbered with heterogeneous associations and historical residues having little, if anything, to do with a strictly liberal democratic *concept* of freedom.

It is pointless, then, to undertake to analyze the liberal democratic concept of freedom by reporting on usages. The term is too rich, usage is too diverse and imprecise, for such descriptive analysis to prove enlightening. As with liberal democratic theory itself, a useful and clear account will of necessity be highly idealized.

In reconstructing the liberal democratic concept of freedom, particular care must be exercised in distinguishing what I shall call the *core concept* from peripheral notions with which the core is characteristically associated, but from which it is logically separable. Doing so will prepare the way (in Part III)—for examining political theories that purport to break from undesirable or theoretically inadequate aspects of traditional liberal positions while retaining conceptual continuity with what is deemed essential to

that tradition. For now, however, the principal objective is to
expose the core concept and some of its presuppositions. It will
turn out that much of what accords least well with our considered
moral intuitions is indeed peripheral, and therfore can be eliminated from a political philosophy that remians, in some very tenuous sense, liberal.

Because freedom is so variously and eclectically understood,
even by liberal democrats, it will be best not to take on that notion
directly, but to focus initially on its more cumbersome, but more
tractable, opposite: *unfreedom*. Precisely because it is so little
invoked,* and therefore less prone to take on heterogeneous associations, unfreedom provides clear and direct access to the liberal democratic concept of freedom. However a note of caution
is advised: in counterposing unfreedom to freedom, I do not mean
to suggest that the core theory includes a notion of an undifferentiated freedom that does not admit of levels or degrees. Liberal
democrats do generally counterpose an undifferentiated freedom
to unfreedom; but, as we shall see, they are not theoretically
obliged to do so. I shall return to this issue in chapter 9, for it is
of some moment in assessing the prospects for a revisionist liberalism. For now, the point is just to expose the core concept. For
that purpose we may suppose, in line with the customary practice
of liberal democrats, that freedom and unfreedom are strictly op-
posites.

Unfreedom

For Kant, and throughout the idealist tradition, freedom (autonomy) and unfreedom (heteronomy) are never conceived as distinctly social or political categories, but rather as metaphysical

---

*The adjective *unfree* is of course common in English; but the noun *unfreedom*
is not entirely natural. Of the philosophical cultures that feed into liberal democratic theory, only the German has a proper word, *Unfreiheit*, for the concept. To
some extent, I think we owe the relative tractability of *unfreedom* to this lack of
a proper word in English or the Romance languages. It is difficult to confound
much into a concept one can hardly talk about.

states of the individual. A proper analysis of these notions, even in specifically political contexts, depends on an account of freedom as such and, therefore, among other things, on a "solution" to the traditional metaphysical problem of the compatibility of free action and casual determination. Liberal democratic writers address these questions also, of course, as John Stuart Mill, for example, did in *An Examination of Sir William Hamilton's Philosophy*. But their account of political freedom does not depend in any important, systematic way on metaphysical accounts of freedom and "solutions" to the problem of free will. This independence of political from metaphysical accounts of freedom is very evident when we consider unfreedom. For as already noted in the last chapter, the liberal democrat construes unfreedom as a social relation, a relation pertaining between persons in society. It is emphatically not, as heteronomy is for Kant, a matter of the casual determination of actions. Persons are unfree only in respect to other persons. A Robinson Crusoe, alone on his island, however much a slave to his passions and therefore "in human bondage" (Spinoza), could never be unfree, so long as there is no one in respect to whom he might be unfree. Unfreedom is an eminently *social* notion.

For this reason, unfreedom is not a psychological state, though it is often, loosely, spoken of as such. Feeling unfree is, at best, only an indication that an unfreedom relation pertains. It is surely not a necessary condition. Thus where there are laws against assault, each person is unfree to assault others (unfree, that is, with respect to the government that enforces the law); but so long as a person has no desire to commit assault, he will likely not feel unfree to do so. Neither is feeling unfree sufficient for being unfree. To take a revealing example (to which we shall return) on which the tradition is insistent: a worker may feel unfree, unsurprisingly, to start his own factory, but so long as there is a free market (and therefore no legal or extra-legal restraints on entrepreneurship), he is not in fact unfree to do so, even if, for all practical purposes, he is unable to become an entrepreneur. If the worker belives himself to be unfree (as distinct from unable), he is mistaken conceptually. Even as an indicator, then, feeling unfree is an unreliable guide.

To be unfree is to be prevented by others from doing what one wants to do.[1] A proper, full-fledged analysis of the concept would focus on determining what counts as rendering persons unfree, on the modalities of preventing persons from doing what they want. However, a finely tuned account is unnecessary here. A rough characterization will suffice.

Many writers in the liberal tradition identify freedom with the absence of *coercion*, and unfreedom, correspondingly, with coercion. Strictly speaking, these identifications are incorrect. Coercion is neither necessary nor sufficient for rendering individuals unfree.[2] To resume our earlier example: if we grant that rendering an action punishable by law, other things being equal, is sufficient for rendering persons unfree to commit that action, then where there are laws against assault, people are unfree to assault one another. But, normally, people are not coerced into not assaulting others. Likewise, one can be coercively restrained from performing some action without being unfree to perform that action. Suppose one person threatens another with a fine should he do x. In fact, however, the threat is a bluff: the person who threatens has no power to exact fines from the person threatened. Nonetheless, the person threatened believes the threat and forbears from doing x because of it. That person was free (not unfree) to do x, but he can fairly be said to have been coerced into not doing x.

Normally, however, coercive restraint is a means for rendering persons unfree: when A is coerced by B to do x, usually, A is rendered unfree by B not to do x. These notions—coercion, unfreedom—overlap considerably, and their putative identification, if not entirely correct, is, as already noted in the last chapter, at least approximately right.

As we know, a sense of the incompatibility of freedom and coercion, particularly coercion by political authorities, is very deeply entrenched in liberal thought. For the liberal, it is profoundly counter-intuitive and even perverse to talk, as Rousseau does, of forcing persons to be free, of coercion for freedom's sake. This opposition—freedom, coercion—even if only approximate, provides a useful point of entry for grasping the liberal concept of freedom.

As generally understood, when B coerces A, B undertakes *deliberate* efforts to cause A to do or forbear from doing some action. Thus coercion generally involves deliberate interference. Where coercion is seen as a principal means for rendering persons unfree—or, more loosely, where being coerced is identified with being unfree—it is natural, again, to suppose that activity that counts as rendering persons unfree must also be deliberate: that if B renders A unfree to do x, B must *intend* to prevent A from doing x. Inadvertently preventing a person from doing what he wants does not render that person unfree. And neither do institutional impediments or interferences, so long as they are not deliberately concocted to have that effect.

Suppose A lives in a society where institutional practices are such that wealth is distributed very unequally (through "impersonal" markets, for example), and where products of labor exchange as commodities at widely varing prices. Then some expensive commodities like jet planes may well be beyond A's means. A is unable to buy a jet plane, then, in virtue of the activities of other persons, so far as these activities constitute the social practices that lead to the distribution of wealth and the pricing of jet planes. These activities are, of course, for the most part deliberate; but their intent is not to prevent A from buying a jet. For this reason, though he is unable to do so, A is free to buy a jet plane. However if the government prohibits, say, convicted felons from owning jet planes, then B, a billionaire convicted embezzler, is, unlike A, unfree (in respect to the government) to buy a jet plane—though, again unlike A, he has the means and is therefore, given the prevailing institutional setting, perfectly able to do so.

There is a major conceptual advantage in this way of construing unfreedom. It allows cases to be sorted out precisely and unambiguously. It is notoriously difficult, if not impossible, to distinguish institutional impediments from natural inabilities. Were institutional impediments to count as rendering persons unfree, along with deliberate interferences, it would be necessary, in order to specify what in fact counts as restricting freedom, to draw a line of demarcation between deliberate interference and institutional impediments, on the one hand, and natural inabilities, on the other. This task, very likely, would prove intractable. However, if institutional impediments are, in effect, assimilated to natural inabilities, so that the line of demarcation is drawn between deliberate interference, on the one hand, and institutional impediments *and* natural inabilities, on the other, the task becomes perfectly tractable and even easy. In addition, in holding that only deliberate interference renders persons unfree, space is left open, as it were, for other values—like justice or equality—in ways that accord tolerably well with our intuitions.[3] That A cannot buy a jet plane or the worker start his own factory, when not attributed just to a lack of success (whether unlucky or deserved) in fair competition, can be blamed on a failure of equality or perhaps justice, but not as a restriction on liberty. It may seem odd, initially, to claim that the rich and poor are equally free to buy jet planes, or that workers are free to start their own factories, but, it could be argued, reflection bears out this way of talking. In any case, the facts of the matter are not in dispute, only how they are to be described. And the liberal democrat could argue, with some plausibility, that the traditional liberal insistence that restrictions on liberty only result from deliberate interferences, provides the most useful and adequate idiom for describing actual situations.

Freedom and the Ends of Man

Very generally, a necessary condition for freedom is the absence of impediments in the pursuit of one's ends. Then to hold, as liberal democrats do, that a person is unfree when prevented (deliberately) by others from doing what he wants, is to suggest a privileged relation between persons and the ends they seek to realize. A person's ends, it seems, are just whatever he takes them to be. It will be necessary, in chapters 3 and 4 to elaborate upon and clarify this claim, and very shortly to qualify it. For the moment, it is enough to note its tremendous impact on shaping liberal democratic theoretical positions. It is because our ends just are what we take them to be that we can never be "forced to be free" by being coerced into pursuing ends not actually held by us, but somehow "discovered" by others. For the liberal democrat, the individual is the final arbiter of his "true" ends. Neither rational standards nor extra-rational information can justify imputing ends to persons and dictating that these imputed ends be actual ends.

But persons, so far as they are rational, are, in this view, utility maximizers. It is assumed, then, that persons are able to order ends quantitatively according to their utility—that is, according to their degree of preference for their realization. In this way, rationality does, after all, impose requirements on ends— not, to be sure, on their content (for, by hypothesis, there are no rational standards by which the contents of ends can be assessed), but on their relations. To say that persons can rank ends according to their utility is to suppose, minimally, that the ends we hold can be ordered. And an ordered set of ends must at least be consistent (transitive).

The rationale for this requirement is readily apparent. If a person orders ends inconsistently (intransitively)—if he prefers x to y and y to z, but z to x, where x, y and z are distinct alternatives—then, in a situation where he is confronted with a choice between all three alternatives, he will find himself unable to act in accordance with his ordering. For any choice he might make, another choice would rank higher acccording to his ordering. If we view an ordering as a program written for oneself qua utility maximizer, an inconsistent ordering provides an impossible program, a program that cannot be acted upon. Thus if one holds ends inconsistently, one cannot maximize utility.

Thus even instrumental reason rules out some orderings of

ends. It proscribes inconsistent orderings. This is a purely formal exclusion, of course, but it is a genuine exclusion nonetheless.

The requirement that orderings be consistent does have an air of unreality. It supposes unlimited powers of discrimination in matters of preference and indifference, an unlikely supposition for human beings, particularly in the case of indifferences. Between x and y, y and z, and z and w, there may be no noticeable difference, so that A is indifferent with respect to any of these pairs. Yet, for A, there may be a noticeable difference between x and w, such that A prefers x to w or w to x. Then, of course, the requirement of consistency (transitivity) would be violated. There is ample evidence that emergent, "just noticeable differences" of this sort are a common feature of human perceptual experience. But however relevant to the analysis of cognition and even of actual choice behavior, this invocation of perceptual thresholds and emergent differences is irrelevant to the analysis of rational agency as it figures in liberal democratic *theory*. There are many reasons why a person's judgment may in fact be inconsistent (intransitive), and some, surely, are cognitive. But consistency (transitivity) is a normative stipulation, not a description of how people in fact order ends. It is an ideal of instrumental reason.

According to that ideal, persons may hold any ends they please, but they may not hold them inconsistently. This is not to deny that reason, as in Hume's expression, is the slave of the passions, but only to indicate how reason serves the passions. To maximize utility, persons must be consistent in their orderings of ends. In requiring this consistency, instrumental reason, as Hume might say, orders the passions so that they may be realized—in accordance with standards that are, strictly, internal to the passions themselves.*

Beyond mere consistency, instrumental reason also requires that, so far as possible, persons act to realize the ends they hold.

*It goes without saying that liberal democrats are not necessarily committed to Hume's moral psychology, nor to his account of "the passions." The term is used here only as a placeholder for whatever dictates our ends. What Hume's expression underscores is that this motivating principle, however construed, is non-rational.

Needless to say, persons may *desire* ends they do not seek to realize. Forbearance from pursuing at least some of our desires is characteristic of (enlightened) utility maximizing behavior, and, no doubt, of any notion of rational and moral agency. But where ends are actively held, where they are *willed*, rational agents will seek to realize them. In Kant's expression, intended to capture this aspect of instrumental reason (in his analysis of "hypothetical" imperatives): to will the end is to will the means thereto.[4]

Correspondence between ends and behavior is at least part of what is usually understood by *prudence*. That persons be prudent, to this extent, is then a further constraint on rational behavior, and so, insofar as we are rational, on our ends. But again, this constraint provides no way to assess ends by standards external to the "passions", that is, to these ends themselves. Our true ends remain just whatever we take them to be. In radical opposition to Kantian and other idealist accounts of rational agency, reason, for the liberal democrat, does no more than *enjoin us to realize the ends we will*. There are, in Kant's terms, only hypothetical, never categorical, imperatives.

Some philosophers have argued that even were reason solely instrumental, there exist ends, like happiness, which are universally willed; all rational agents will the means to these ends. This is at least one way of understanding what Kant calls "counsels of prudence." Others have suggested that whatever a person's ends might be, there exist certain "primary goods" that are always instrumental to their attainment.* Then any rational agent would will these primary goods, whatever his particular ends. In these ways, it is sometimes maintained that at least some ends actually are enjoined by instrumental reason, even if there are no rational standards against which the content of our ends may be assessed.

On a sufficiently grand level of generality, it may well be that all people will happiness. But then happiness would have to be understood so broadly—encompassing, at once, the happiness of

---

*The expression is of course John Rawls', but the idea is implicit in Locke's account of the social contract.

saints and sinners—that no specific means will be enjoined for each person. So far as different things make different people happy, good advice, counsels of prudence, will be universally applicable only to the degree they are vacuous. On the other hand, the claim that primary goods exist, while not empty, is very likely false—so long as we adhere to a view of reason as only instrumental. For each of the putative primary goods, one can easily imagine ends for which they are not functional or for which they are even disfunctional. Thus wealth, good health and self-esteem, while certainly instrumental for the attainment of many particular ends and the realization of most life plans, are hardly instrumental for any end a person might will. Those who, for reasons deemed "spiritual," seek to lead lives of self-deprivation and self-abasement would likely have no use for these goods, and might even find them obstacles in the way of fulfilling their life plans. And these ends, at least for liberal democrats, cannot be discounted as irrational, inasmuch as reason does not rule on the content of our ends.

But even if, as seems unlikely, there are non-vacuous consels of prudence or universally useful primary goods, these ends are not enjoined by instrumental reason as such, but by a common experience of human beings. They are, as Kant might say, contingent, not necessary, ends; even should they, as a matter of fact, be universally willed. It is *possible* that a rational agent could fail to will these ends, even if it were the case that none did. For these ends are not enjoined by reason as such, but elicited, as it were, by the situation in which reasonable beings find themselves.

We see, then, that while instrumental reason is not indifferent to our ends, it offers no standards against which the content of our ends may be assessed. Reason, the slave, must accommodate, ultimately, to its master's caprice.

A person's *true ends*, in this view, are just those ends he would entertain given full knowledge and adequate reflection. Presumably, the perfectly rational (prudent) person will always will his true ends. (Indeed, we might say that correspondence between actual and true ends, along with correspondence between actual ends and behavior, constitute *prudence*.)[5] However, persons often fail to will their true ends; knowledge and reflection are often inadequate. And, at least sometimes, others may be better able than the agents themselves to ascertain what the agent's true ends are. To be sure, as Mill insists, each person may in general be the best judge of his own interests.[6] But where there is conclusive or even very good evidence to the contrary, shouldn't this information be used to *correct* the agent's own assessments and, if need be, shouldn't the agent be *forced* to do what he *really wants*? In other words, even with the notion of rational agency liberal democrats suppose, doesn't it still make sense to talk of forcing persons to be free?

The traditional answer is, of course, negative. However, it is not entirely clear why. John Stuart Mill, the least dogmatic of orthodox liberals, seems to acknowledge the possibility of an affirmative answer, while insisting that in practice any intervention of this sort is likely to turn out poorly, and so, as a matter of social policy, should generally be avoided.[7] More often, though, liberal writers just take for granted that a person is rendered unfree by others—when prevented by someone's deliberate activity from doing what he wants—even if the other's intent is only to force the person to do what he *would* want, or might reasonably be thought to want, given full knowledge and adequate reflection. A person's judgments, for the liberal democrat, are radically incorrigible, though they may of course be imprudent. To attribute ends to persons, even *true* ends, is not to force persons to be free, but— even if for their own good—to restrict their liberty.

There may of course be circumstances where individuals are compelled *justifiably* to do what others discern to be their true interests. Liberalism can and does accommodate a measure of paternalism. But whenever paternalistic interference is countenanced, it counts as a restriction on liberty. Thus were the government to require alcoholics or drug addicts to undergo rehabilitative treatment, if need be against their will, the government would be rendering such persons unfree to fail to undergo the treatment (even if, in so doing, it were only forcing such people to do what they would do voluntarily, were they fully capable of discerning their true ends). Sometimes restrictions on liberty of this sort are justified on expressly paternalistic grounds, by appeal to the person's interest. More often, the appeal is to society's interest. In either case, there is, *pace* Mill, a trade-off between utility and liberty. Persons may be forced to do what is best, for themselves or others, but they are not thereby forced to be free. In the final analysis, every agent determines his own ends; everyone is the final judge of what his ends are. Whether in particular cases each agent is also the best, or even a good, judge may be a vital question for many purposes, including determination of social policy. But imprudence is not unfreedom, and forcing a person to act prudently is not forcing him to be free.

Freedom and Institutions

A consequence of the stipulation that only deliberate interference can render persons unfree is, as already noted, a tendency to abstract from institutional practices and arrangements in considerations of freedom. Institutional impediments to persons' doing what they want, so long as they are not deliberately contrived to be impediments, do not render persons unfree. Freedom is just the absence of unfreedom relations. To maximize freedom, then, is nothing more nor less than to minimize unfreedom, to minimize deliberate interference with persons' doing what they want. So far as freedom is concerned, all else is irrelevant.

   Can this stipulation be detached from the core concept? Can we maintain a liberal concept of freedom without requiring that only deliberate interferences render persons unfree? The answer we settle upon is important, as we shall see, for many further questions to be considered in what follows: among others, whether freedom must include the sorts of "economic freedoms" characteristic of capitalist, but apparently not socialist, political economic arrangements (basically, freedom to buy and sell labor power), and whether it is possible in principle to go "beyond liberalism," while retaining its core concept of freedom. We have already seen that there are at least two considerations that might be advanced on behalf of this stipulation: it facilitates drawing clear distinctions between what restricts liberty and what does not, and it provides space for other moral ideals in assessing social and political arrangements. On the other side, this stipulation, it might be thought, is blatantly counter-intuitive and, insofar as it tends to protect existing institutional arrangements from criticism, ideologically conservative. But however compelling these considerations may be, they do not address the question at hand: whether this stipulation, whatever its merits or defects, is conceptually detachable from the rest of what comprises the liberal democrat's notion of freedom.

I would maintain that this stipulation is indeed detachable, that the view that it is not rests on a confusion, and that even this confusion depends less on the liberal concept of freedom than on a deep and pervasive individualism that has played an important role throughout the history of liberal democratic thought, but is itself detachable from liberal democratic theory. I shall call the form of individualism that is pertinent here *atomic individualism* because its character is best brought out by analogy with early atomistic theories of matter. For atomic individualists, the ultimate constituents of social reality, the atoms, are individual men and women, essentially independent of one another and of society, bearing only extrinsic relations to one another. Like atoms in an enclosed space, individuals in society do come into contact with one another. But this contact is in no way constitutive of the individual's nature. Society no more constitutes individuals than space constitutes atoms. Physical space is just where atoms are collected. Society, similarly, is just a collection of (atomic) individuals. Society is no more a part of social reality than physical space, in the traditional atomist view, is part of matter.

That this view of society is indeed peripheral and therefore detachable conceptually from liberal democracy's core theory will be argued in chapter 4. For now, it will be enough to trace an effect of atomic individualism upon liberal democratic theory: its role in motivating the contentious stipulation in question here. My claim is that the requirement that only deliberate interference renders persons unfree derives its plausibility from liberal democracy's characteristic atomic individualism.

For the atomic individualist, associations of any sort, and a fortiori institutional practices and arrangements, are always only instrumental. Such associations are logically subordinate to individuals and their purposes. Accordingly, either an institution is somehow non-rational and therefore unintelligible, or else it has, so to speak, a sufficient reason given in terms of the maximizing behavior of atomic individuals. Within the tradition that regards rationality as Hobbes did, the absence of a sufficient reason for individuals' behaviors is abhorrent. Indeed, it is this abhorrence of unintelligibility that provides the rationale, for Hobbes and even Locke, for the contractarian program, according to which institutions are *justified* to the extent that they are in every person's interest, where persons are depicted in suitably characterized "states of nature" (from which the arrangements in question are abstracted). But the account of (human) motivation on which this program rests is more general, pertaining not only to justifiable institutional arrangements, but to all institutions, including those, justifiable or not, that render persons unfree.

In all cases, what motivates institutional arrangements are the ends willed by atomic individuals. In this sense, arrangements that restrict liberty can hardly fail to be deliberate. So far as an account can be given, there is always a (deliberate) motive to be discovered.

But how is this motive to be ascertained? If we allow rational reconstructions, then the requirement that restrictions on liberty be deliberate is, effectively, trivialized. If all institutional arrangements are instrumental and *thereby* deliberate, so must be those that restrict liberty. But, as we have seen, this result is implemented in a way that is anything but trivial, that rules out all unintended institutional impediments to persons doing what they want. In other words, rational reconstructions are disallowed, after all, in favor of only those motives that are actually entertained.

What has happened, apparently, is that for institutions, "deliberate" is understood simultaneously in two distinct senses. On the one hand, an institutional arrangement is deliberate insofar as it is intelligible, insofar as a motive for it can be imputed to atomic individuals by rational reconstruction. On the other hand, an instituion arrangement counts as an impediment only if it is actually intended to prevent someone from doing something. On the former understanding of "deliberate," it follows trivially that only deliberate interferences restrict liberty. On the latter understanding, it does not follow at all. Yet liberal democrats do generally hold that only deliberate interferences render persons unfree, and their understanding of this claim is anything but trivial in its applications. It seems that insofar as this view is warranted at all, its rationale rests on conflating these senses of "deliberate," using the argument, such as it is, for what is trivially true to justify what is very contentious.

I would suggest, therefore, that what finally requires explanation is just the persistence of this view, its tenacity, despite its apparent lack of justification. But to pursue that line of inquiry would be to investigate the ideological bearing of liberal democratic positions, positions that effectively minimize and even deny the role of institutional arrangements in considerations pertinent to political philosophy. I will return to this issue in Part III.

In Part III also, I shall consider how liberal democrats might allow consideration of degrees of freedom, and, more important for the critique of liberal democratic theory, speculate why, for the most part, liberal democrats don't. This question too touches on the ideological bearing of liberal democratic theory.

For now, the point is just to sketch the core concept. We can already see that liberal democracy's characteristic stipulation that restrictions on liberty be deliberate belongs to the periphery, not the core, of the concept. In principle, therefore, it is eliminable. And so too, it would seem, is liberal democracy's characteristic abstraction from institutional arrangements. It seems that there is ample room for revising liberal democratic theory—retaining the core, while rejecting, among other things, liberal democracy's characteristic abstractness and neglect of social reality. Even so, I will argue in Part III that the prospects for a successful revisionist liberalism—adequate in its own right and genuinely continuous conceptually with the liberal democratic tradition—are grim.

3 / Interests

THE democratic component of liberal democratic theory is justified, implicitly, on aggregative grounds. The point is to maximize interest satisfaction, and democratic collective choice rules are means to that end. Thus liberal democratic theory rests upon a particular notion of interest, reducible, as already indicated, to non- or extra-rational wants or desires. Liberal democrats, of course, talk of interests in other senses as well: of interests reducible to needs (independent of wants) or of interests as ideal standards of what is good for a person (again, independent of persons' wants). But it is, I have maintained, the strictly want-regarding sense that underlies and motivates what is distinctive in the democratic component. In this chapter, this claim will be elaborated upon and expanded. Of particular concern will be the liberal democrat's commitment to majority rule voting as a means for maximizing interest satisfaction, and also liberal democracy's use of notions of "the public interest."

Combining Interests

We have seen how the liberal democrat's commitment to further individuals' (private) interests is tantamount to investing sovereignty in collective decision procedures of certain sorts—ideally, in majority rule voting. The basic intuition, again, is that the form of sovereignty that accords best with individuals' interests is one that does only what *the people,* conceived as a collection of individual voters, want it to do. The social choice should just be a combination of the choices of those who constitute the political community. Thus the sovereign people express their will by combining individual choices to produce social choices. And majority rule seems the best way to bring this combination about, because it is the decision procedure least biased for or against some enactment, and therefore, most responsive to individuals' choices.

Sovereignty, then, can be represented as a "legislature" where citizens vote on matters pertaining to public policy. Thus, as already noted, the core theory of (liberal) democracy suggests direct democratic control, just as Rousseau did for the ideal state of *The Social Contract*. Rousseau insisted that sovereignty was indivisible and could not be represented. The core theory of liberal democracy virtually concedes these theses, and then proceeds, in marked contrast to Rousseau's strictures, to advocate "dividing" sovereignty among a number of "branches" of representative government. This emendation of the core theory is not, I will contend (in chapter 8), simply an accommodation to the practical difficulties involved in assembling the entire people as a legislature and collecting their votes. The recourse to representative institutions, in the face of the core theory, is, I will argue, the key to understanding the historical feasibility of the liberal democratic project. But our concern for now is with the pure theory, and not yet with its practical implementations.

The process of legislating may be reconstructed as a collective choice rule, a device for mapping individuals' choices into social choices.[1] Suppose there exists a set of (mutually exclusive) candidates for social choice. And suppose too that individuals order these alternatives according to their degree of preference (or indifference) for their realization.* Then taking these orderings as inputs, the legislative process may be represented as in figure 3.1.

---

*Let R be the ordering relation, read ". . . is preferred or indifferent to . . ." and x, y, and z be alternatives in contention. Then for all x, y, and z, xRy and yRz imply xRz (transitivity); for all x and y, either xRy or yRx (connectedness); and for all x, xRx (reflexivity). Transitivity reconstructs consistency; connectedness and reflexivity stipulate that a choice be made among discrete alternatives.

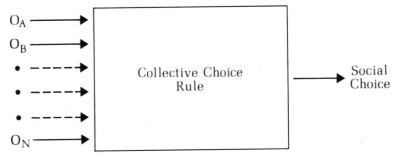

Figure 3.1

The inputs $O_a, O_b, ..., O_n$ represent the orderings of individuals a,b,...,n. The collective choice rule combines these orderings to produce a social choice, itself an ordering of the alternatives in contention. Characteristically, each individual's ordering counts equally in the determination of the social choice. No differential weights are assigned to individuals' orderings; there are as many inputs as there are voters.

It is reasonable to stipulate that any collective choice rule that counts as democratic will satisfy the following conditions:

Collective Rationality. For any logically possible individual orderings, the collective choice rule determines an ordering for the society.

Weak Pareto Principle. If one alternative is ranked higher than another by all individuals, according to their orderings, that alternative will rank higher in the social ordering.

Independence of Irrelevant Alternatives. For any set of alternative outcomes, the social choice depends only on the individuals' orderings of the alternatives in contention.

Non-Dictatorship. There is no individual whose choices are automatically society's choices, regardless of the choices of all other individuals.

These conditions appear to be minimal and eminently reasonable. Nonetheless, as Kenneth Arrow has demonstrated, they are mutually inconsistent; a decision procedure satisfying all four conditions simultaneously is "impossible."

Let us call a decision procedure that satisfies each of these mutually inconsistent conditions an *Arrow social welfare function*.* Plainly, majority rule voting is an Arrow social welfare function, one that requires that X be chosen over y whenever the number of individuals who choose x over y is greater than the number who choose y over x. In majority rule voting, a simple numerical majority is decisive for or against an outcome. Very often, social choices are in fact made by majority rule, just as they are by other decision procedures that are Arrow social welfare functions. What can it mean, then, to say that Arrow social welfare functions or, more particularly, majority rule voting procedures are "impossible"? What does the impossibility of majority rule amount to?

The point is plainly not that majority rule voting somehow fails to produce social choices. Majority rule does produce social choices. What Arrow has shown is that these choices may be produced in ways that violate one or another of the stipulated conditions.

The failure to satisfy four conditions simultaneously will be evident in *cyclical* majorities, where the alternatives that are chosen over other alternatives are not socially preferred, according to the orderings of the individual voters. This situation is illustrated by the celebrated voting paradox. Suppose there are three alternatives in contention, x, y, and z and three voters, A, B, and C. Voter A prefers x to y and y to z, and therefore x to z. Voter B

---

*Majority rule voting is only one of many *impossible* decision procedures that satisfy Arrow's conditions. So too do voting procedures requiring larger than simple numerical majorities; and some non-voting procedures (for example, "free markets"). To opt for majority rule voting, then, is to choose a decision procedure of some particularity. It was argued in chapter 1 that this choice in fact accords best with the intuitions that motivate liberal democracy's commitment to popular sovereignty.

prefers y to z and z to x, and therefore y to x. Voter C prefers z to x and x to y and therefore z to y. If we consider alternatives pairwise and vote according to the method of majority rule, there will always be a winner. Thus if we begin by comparing x and y, x will win, since the majority (in this case, voters A and C) prefer x to y. Then if we pair x, the winner, against the remaining alternative z, z wins (since both B and C prefer z to x), and the social ordering, therefore, is z–x–y. However, as can be readily seen, if we begin by comparing x and z, and then pair the winner off against the remaining alternative y, the social ordering will be y–z–x; and if we begin with y and z, the social ordering will be x–y–z. Every alternative, then, is preferred to every other alternative or, what comes to the same thing, majority rule voting does not produce a unique, transitive social ordering (appearance to the contrary). The problem, of course, is not that majority rule will *always* yield cyclical social choices, but that it *can* (depending on the orderings to be combined). It is worth noting that when the number of alternatives is large, so too is the probability of cyclical outcomes.[3]

The impossibility (incoherence) of Arrow social welfare functions, and thus of majority rule voting, would seem to have devastating consequences for liberal democratic theory or, more strictly, for its democratic component. The democratic component can hardly be defended for maximizing interest satisfaction, if it is itself literally incoherent, and if its incoherence is manifest in collective choices that may not in fact be socially preferred. In Arrow's formulation, our intuitions about democratic choice are captured by the Weak Pareto Principle and the Non-Dictatorship conditions. (Collective Rationality and the Independence of Irrelevant Alternatives, while hardly innocent, as we shall see presently, function to formulate the problem of social choice, rather than to capture our intuitions about democratic choice.) The Weak Pareto Principle and the Non-Dictatorship conditions, while plainly not sufficient for reconstructing democratic choice, are surely necessary. The Weak Pareto Principle requires only that whenever all voters prefer x to y, the social ordering should rank x above y. The Non-Dicatorship condition requires only that no individual be able to dictate the social orderings, that is, that no individual's choice automatically be the social choice. No collective choice rule that violates these conditions could possibly count as democratic. Yet whenever an aggregating mechanism satisfies these conditions, along with Collective Rationality and the Independence of Irrelevant Alternatives, that mechanism is, formally, incoherent!

In the extensive literature Arrow's work has stimulated, it is most common to try to avoid incoherence by tampering with one or another of the conditions on Collective Rationality and the Independence of Irrelevant Alternatives. The role of these conditions, as already noted, is more to formulate the problem of social choice than to express our intuitions about democratic choice. If the impossibility of majority rule voting, and of other Arrow social welfare functions, is to be overcome by changing either or both of these conditions, there must be something wrong, or at least inappropriate, about the way Arrow's formulation rationally reconstructs the collective choice problem.

Collective Rationality is, in fact, an amalgam of two distinct claims: that the society have a consistent (transitive) ordering of the alternatives in contention, and that the individual voters whose choices are to be combined may order the alternatives in any way they please, so long as they do so consistently. To abandon the first of these claims is not to solve the problem, but to decide, without good reason, to overlook it. That a consistent social ordering be produced is a reasonable requirement for a collective choice rule for the same reason that consistency, as noted in chapter 2, is a reasonable requirement for individuals seeking to maximize utility. To see why, it is useful to consider an intransitive ordering as a command—say, from a master to a servant. The servant is instructed to do x rather than y, y rather than z, but z rather than x. In this event, faced with a choice between x, y, and z, there is no way for the servant to do the master's will. The intransitivity of the master's ordering renders the command he issues impossible to fulfill. The master's command is incoherent. Therefore, whatever the servant does cannot be strictly in accord with it. The same consideration holds for social orderings, whenever, as in the core theory of the democratic component, the point is to command "public servants"—officials obliged to enact the will of the majority. Intransitive orderings render this mission impossible to realize. The public servant cannot enact the social choice when, strictly speaking, there is no (coherent) social choice, even if there is a winner in every vote. To tamper with this aspect of Collective Rationality, then, is to tamper with the rationale for majority rule voting in liberal democratic theory. A liberal democrat can hardly do that.

What remains, then, if Collective Rationality is to be the culprit, is to impose restrictions on individual orderings: to modify the stipulation that the choice mechanism produce an ordering from *any* logically possible input. There is, in fact, a substantial literature devoted to just this strategy.[4] The idea is not to proscribe orderings *a priori*; to do so would be recklessly undemocratic. Rather, the idea is to require that there be structural relations among the orderings to be combined, patterns of "similarity" that reconstruct consensus not on the orderings themselves, but on the bases according to which these orderings are formed. It can be shown, for example, that if condition 1 is modified to admit only "single-peaked" orderings, rather than any orderings whatsoever, there is no incoherence; that conditions 2—4 and condition I, modified as indicated, are consistent.[5] Single-peaked orderings are those that can be represented on a graph with the rank of preference on the ordinate and the alternatives themselves arranged along the abscissa, such that a representation of each individual's ordering has only one peak. Thus if alternatives x, y, and z are arranged in the order x,y,z along the abscissa, and if voter A prefers x to y and y to z (and therefore x to z), if voter B prefers y to z and z to x (and therefore y to x), and if voter C prefers z to y and y to x (and therefore z to x), each individual's ordering is single-peaked, as can be seen from figure 3.2, and there is a unique, non-cyclical social choice, y–z–x, as can be readily seen.

To see what may happen if the set of orderings to be combined

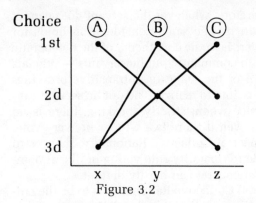

Figure 3.2

is not single-peaked,* suppose voter C's ordering has been z–x–y. We would then have the set of orderings that gave rise to the voting paradox. In this case, there is no arrangement of the alternatives x, y, and z along the abscissa of a graph that would be such that each individual's ordering could be represented by a single-peaked graph. This claim is easily verified by observation. In figure 3.3 each of the possible arrangements of the alternatives is shown along with the ordering that violates the requirement of single-peakedness. As we know, for this set of orderings, majority rule voting does not yield a unique social ordering. Rather, every alternative is preferred to every other; the outcome is cyclical.

It seems intuitively plausible that the dimension along which individual's orderings are single-peaked, wherever such a dimension exists, represents a (probably implicit) consensus on standards according to which individuals assess alternatives. Thus while voters may not agree on actual choices, they might at least agree on how choices are to be evaluated, as when voters effectively arrange themselves along a generally accepted left-right political spectrum. In other words, it seems that agreement on how alternatives are to be judged—a requirement a good deal

---

*It should be stressed that single-peakedness, while sufficient, is not necessary for avoiding Arrow's result. Inputs that are not single-peaked can also give rise to unique, transitive social choices.

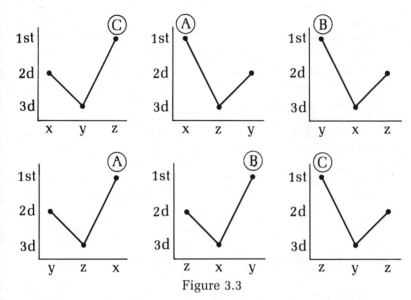

Figure 3.3

weaker than actual agreement on alternatives—is sufficient for avoiding Arrow's result.

In general, results of this sort are of interest for political philosophy to the extent they reconstruct moves actually made in political arguments or anticipate moves that might be made. For this reason, it is unlikely that the liberal democrat will fund much consolation in restricting inputs to social welfare functions, whether to single-peaked orderings or to those satisfying any of the other host of intuitively less appealing restrictions that have been proposed in the considerable literature on the subject. At least where atomic individualist views of society remain influential, and particularly where the long-enshrined goal of encouraging individual differences, enthusiastically advocated by Mill in *On Liberty*, remains in force, there is every reason to suppose that idiosyncratic standards for evaluating alternatives will supercede any tendency for the universal adoption of common standards.* And without good reason to expect the universal adoption of common standards, there is no good reason, it seems, to restrict the domain of individuals' orderings. It is not surprising, then, that the technical literature on restricting inputs, so far at least, is not even remotely helpful for liberal democrats who would avoid Arrow's result. It is fair to speculate that there is little prospect of help from this quarter.

The Independence of Irrelevant Alternatives has been perhaps the most disputed of Arrow's conditions. Much of the controversy it has elicited, however, is the result of misunderstandings about what it requires; misunderstandings encouraged by some of Arrow's comments in *Social Choice and Individual Values*. These misunderstandings need not detain us here.† Properly understood, the condition calls just for a fixed set of options in contention. For such a fixed set, the stipulation is that changes in individuals' orderings of options not actually in contention (irrelevant alternatives) have no effect on the social ordering of alternatives actually in contention (relevant alternatives), *so long as these changes have no effect on the individuals' orderings of relevant alternatives*. In other words, the condition requires only that the social ordering be determined by the individuals' order-

---

*Strictly speaking, Mill encourages *private* idiosyncracies, saying nothing that would suggest advocacy of idiosyncratic standards in arriving at collective choices. But it is reasonable to anticipate a spill-over. Certainly Millean individualists would be less likely than more conformist types to view alternatives according to the same criteria.

†Arrow, *Social Choice and Individual Values, op. cit.*, pp. 26-28. The misleading impression Arrow gives is that the condition requires that voters' choices be unaffected by their preferences (and indifferences) for alternatives not in contention. This claim is plainly unrealistic. For example, if a person must choose a pet from among dogs, cats, and rabbits, his desire for a chimpanzee (an alternative, let us say, not in contention) may affect his ordering of the three "relevant" alternatives (it may even make him indifferent with respect to all three). It is surely plausible that his ordering might be different were chimpanzees out of mind, as well as out of contention. Yet some of Arrow's comments on this condition seem to deny this kind of dependence on "irrelevant alternatives." However, as discussed above, the Independence of Irrelevant Alternatives, properly understood, makes no claim about how individual choices are formed, but only about how individuals' choices should be treated, once they are formed.

ings of relevant alternatives. It makes no claim whatsoever about how these orderings are themselves formed. Thus the Independence of Irrelevant Alternatives does no more than help to formulate the problem under investigation. It stipulates that the collective decision rule aggregate individual choices *among a fixed set of options* to produce a social choice *among those options*. (In virtue of Collective Rationality, this social choice, like the individual choices out of which it is formed, is an ordering). This condition, again, makes no claim about how individuals' orderings are formed. It only requires that, for generating social choices out of individuals' choices, these orderings, however formed, should be treated as given, and as the exclusive ground for the social choice.

An objection sometimes leveled against the Independence of Irrelevant Alternatives maintains that it precludes the very possibility of representing information relevant to assessments of social welfare. Arrow's formulation of the problem of social choice is *ordinalist*; alternatives are ranked first, second, third, and so on, by both individuals and society. These rankings, then, cannot represent information about preference intensity (degree of utility). Ordinalists can represent the information that x is preferred to y, and y is preferred to z; but not, say, that x is vastly preferred to y, while y is only slightly preferred to z.

Yet such information, if accessible, is surely relevant ot welfare assessments. (Doubt about the accessibility of this indisputably relevant information is a principal motivation for ordinalist analyses of individual and social choices by economists and others). Moreover, were individual choices represented by cardinal utility functions, assigning cardinal numbers (1, 2, 3 and so on) to alternatives in such a way as to measure prefernce intensity, and were these measures somehow interpersonally comparable, then not only would welfare assessments be sounder for taking account of relevant information, but there would be no problem in aggregating individuals' choices. Once the proper measurements were made, they could be combined simply by adding them together. The classical utilitarian analysis of social welfare thus avoids Arrow's result at the same time that it captures our intuitions about social welfare better, it seems, than ordinalists can.

Needless to say, the apparently intractable difficulties in making the requisite measurements—in constructing cardinal utility functions for individuals and then in comparing the resulting utility assignments interpersonally—work against this "solution" to the problem. But, the argument runs, were these measurement problems somehow overcome, as seems at least conceivable, we ought to analyse welfare cardinally, as classical utilitarians do, not ordinally, and we therefore should not preclude the very possibility of a utilitarian solution by the conditions we stipulate for the social welfare function. But, technically, utilitarian solutions are precluded by the Independence of Irrelevant Alternatives. To establish the appropriate metric, a baseline would have to be determined; and this baseline would be an irrelevant alternative of the sort this condition rules out. Therefore, as widely formulated, the Independence of Irrelevant Alternatives would have to be viewed as an unacceptable condition by utilitarians or indeed by anyone who regards cardinal analyses of social welfare to be at least possible, if not yet (or ever) feasible.

However this objection, though arguably well-taken for traditional formulations of the condition, has no bearing on the present problem.[6] The aggregating mechanisms important for the democratic component are not devices for combining individual welfare assessments but voting procedures (indeed, typically, simple majority rule voting procedures). The Independence of Irrelevant Alternatives, so far as it precludes cardinal analyses of welfare, may indeed be inadequate for capturing all we might want to include under social welfare, but it surely is adequate for reconstructing the problem of collective choice in liberal democracy.

As Arrow's formulation makes clear, within the conceptual framework that produces liberal democratic theory, these notions—social welfare, democratic collective choice—are very closely linked. They are each ways of combining individuals' interests (in the sense appropriate for liberal democratic theory). But these notions are not quite the same. What matters for the democratic component is in a sense the aggregative maximum, social welfare; but *under conditions of democratic collective choice.*

It does appear, then, that the mechanism for combining interests proper to liberal democratic theory, majority rule voting and its close approximations, is profoundly defective. Plainly, the bearing of this conclusion on the core theory is devastating. The democratic component cannot be relied upon to do what its defenders claim for it. In chapter 5, yet another impossibility result will be considered. These demonstrations of incoherence must somehow be addressed. A political theory that passes them over is like a system of applied geometry that countenances circles that can be transformed into squares. The theory may be workable under some conditions or for some purposes. But it is fatally flawed. In chapter 8, we shall examine liberal democracy's attempts to square the circle.

To forestall misunderstandings, it will be useful, very briefly, to emphasize what the argument begun here does *not* purport to show.

To say that majority rule voting is "impossible" is not to say that cyclical majorities of the sort the voting paradox illustrates will frequently arise in actual voting situations. In fact, political representation and the panoply of parliamentary procedures and trade-offs that come with it *do* effectively minimize the actual impact of cyclical majorities. However the claim of incoherence introduced here is not directed against the actual functioning of liberal democratic institutions, but against the *theory* that ultimately justifies these institutions. The point is that the theory of liberal democracy, or more strictly of its democratic component, insofar as it depends on an "impossible" collective choice rule, is radically defective. For this reason, it is not just implausible but quite beside the point to argue that incoherence notwithstanding, the democratic component of liberal democratic theory authorizes a reasonable or desirable form of political organization, or at least the best of the feasible alternatives. The problem is that its theory is defective, neither more nor less.

If the aggregative maximum cannot in general be achieved the way liberal democratic theory requires, the rationale for the democratic component is undone. What is put in question is precisely the investiture of sovereignty in the people, popular sovereignty. It will be recalled that the liberal democrat, in effect, subscribes to Hobbesian arguments for sovereignty (though not to Hobbes' account of the character or limits of sovereign power): the establishment of sovereignty is the sole reasonable alternative, in view of individuals' interests, to the war of all against all. But then the liberal democrat goes beyond Hobbes, to address the question of the form of sovereignty. In a move that is apparently at odds with its underlying conception of politics (see chapter 1), the liberal democrat goes on to hold, again to promote individuals' interests, that the sovereign be the people themselves, organized as a "legislature," to enact those measures that best realize their interests. It is this move beyond Hobbes, the move that joins Hobbism with the democratic tradition, that the demonstrated impossibility of majority rule undermines. It seems that the Hobbesian foundations for the democratic component will not adequately support a commitment to democratic collective choice.

The Public Interest

The result just explored is unintuitive and, prior to recent investigation of collective choice, unexpected. Even today, common sense militates against an appreciation of majority rule's conceptual difficulties; it remains contentious to suggest that its commitment to majority rule voting is somehow a problem for liberal democratic theory. However there are some related concepts, of importance in contemporary political life, that are immediately troublesome for liberal democrats. Chief among these is the concept of the *public interest*. What role can the public interest play in liberal democratic theory?

Individuals' interests are expressed in their choices for alternative options in contention in individual or collective decision-making. The whole community too is thought to have interests; its interests are whatever its democratic collective choice rule generates as output (taking expressions of individuals' interests as input). Sometimes liberal democrats identify the public interest with this societal interest, with what Rousseau pejoratively called "the will of all." Then the concept of the public interest is neither more nor less problematic than the concept of democratic collective choice, and justifications for government acting in the public interest amount to justifications for majoritarianism or its close approximations. Particularly in the last century, it was commonplace to argue that there is no public interest apart from the will of all. Thus Bentham: "The community is a fictitious *body*, compoased of the individual persons who are considered as constituting as it were its *members*. The interest of the community then is, what?—the sum of the interests of the several members who compose it."[7]

The first liberal democrats, if they talked of the public interest at all, generally did identify it with the will of all, and the impression that liberal democracy cannot countenance any other notion of the public interest has persisted to this day, at least for some of liberalism's critics.[8] Plainly, to identify the public interest with the will of all is tantamount to denying that liberal democratic theory has a proper notion of the public interest, at least in the sense that the term has in much contemporary political discussion. Installing air pollution devices in automobiles is the kind of measure often claimed, with relatively little controversy, to be in the public interest. But the installation of air pollution devices is very likely not the will of all, and those who advocate such measures in the name of the public interest would hardly claim that it was.

Moreover, talk of public interests different from the will of all has become increasingly prominent, both in actual political discourse and in political theory. Is such talk simply confused or disingenuous, presenting particular interests as the public interest with a view to mobilizing the support of the gullible or unwitting?

Very often, undoubtedly, the answer is yes. Claims that a given measure is or is not in the public interest ought, indeed, to be greeted with considerable scepticism. But there is, nonetheless, an account of the public interest that can be given within liberal democratic theory, at least if we bracket the aggregation problem. Since, finally, the aggregation problem cannot be bracketed, the concept is a troubled one, but I shall argue that it is a good deal less troubled than the will of all.

Confusion arises, in part, because "the public" is held to designate *everybody*, to be synonymous with "the whole community."[9] However, this understanding is at odds with the usage that is commonplace in legal discourse and, increasingly, even in social philosophy where "the public" designates not everybody, but *anybody*. Here is a definition of the adjective *public*, revived recently by Brian Barry, but formulated nearly a century and a half ago:

Public, as opposed to *private*, is that which has no immediate relation to any specified person or persons, but may directly concern any member or members of the community, without distinction. Thus the acts of a magistrate, or a member of a legislative assembly, done by them in those capacities, are called public; the acts done by the same persons towards their family or friends, or in their dealing with strangers for their own peculiar purposes, are called private. So a theatre, or a place of amusement, is said to be public, not because it is actually visited by every member of the community, but because it is open to all indifferently; and any person may, if he desire, enter it. The same remark applies to public houses, public inns, public meetings, etc. The publication of a book is the exposing of it to sale in such a manner that it may be procured by any person who desires to purchase it: it would be equally public, if not a single copy were sold. In the language of our law, public appear to be distinguished from private acts of parliament on the grounds that the one class directly affects the whole community, the other some definite person or persons.[10]

The *public*, in short, is *anybody;* the *whole community* is *everybody*. The terms are easily confused, but they are distinct conceptually.

What, then, is to be made of "the public interest"? The obvious answer is that the public interest is the interest of individuals *as members of the public,* and that the public interest then differs from "the will of all" in just the way that the public differs from the whole community. But what is it to speak of the interests of an unspecified group of persons, the public?

Actual political discourse is, we know, often confused and ambiguous in its uses of "interest." Claims about persons' or groups' interests very often are claims about what is good for persons or groups, according to some standard independent of individuals' wants. I have already insisted that this use of "interest," however widespread, is strictly foreign to liberal democratic theory. In the next chapter, we shall see that such ideal-regarding uses of "interest" rest upon a view of practical reason incompatible with what underlies both liberalism and that strain of democratic theory that joins with it to form liberal democratic theory. The ideal-regarding sense of "interest" is *not* the liberal democratic concept, even if it is often employed, implicitly or explicitly, by liberal democratic writers. The liberal democratic concept, accordingly, cannot be understood to stand for what is good for the public. If there is a proper liberal democratic concept of the public interest, it must have to do instead with what the public wants.

Tentatively, what the public wants is what the individuals who form the public want *as members of the public.* Here it is important not to confound a distinction that is tenable within a liberal democratic framework with a superficially similar, but in fact quite different distinction, drawn in various ways within idealist political philosophy. For liberal democrats, it is entirely proper to imagine individuals considering alternative options or policies from the point of view of the public, abstracting from their particular wants as "assignable" individuals and assessing options for the public at large (of course, including themselves). Viewing alternatives from the public point of view, one might, for example, opt in favor of constructing a highway upon which one will never travel and from which one will likely derive no discernible benefit; one might choose policies favorable to the arts, though one takes no interest in the arts, and so on. In so doing, alternatives are not assessed according to standards independent of persons' wants, and certainly not according to any notion of what reason requires. In choosing as members of the public, individuals are not aiming (as Rousseau would have the citizens of a just state aim) at a general interest, understood to be each individual's true interest as a citizen, regardless of his wants as a person. For the liberal democrat, in the final analysis, interests are reducible to wants. But these wants can be assessed and evaluated from public, as well as strictly private, perspectives.

Needless to say, there remains the problem of combining the choices of individuals as members of the public. This problem, as in the more general case where individuals assess alternatives according to any point of view whatsoever, is of course nugatory when all individuals agree.* Measures or policies unanimously selected by individuals choosing as members of the public, are therefore clear and unproblematic instances of measures or policies in the public interest. Many putative *public goods*, such as provisions for national defense or for public health, are thought to be *common interests* of this sort, shared interests of individuals as members of the public. So too are the various negative applications of the public interest—as when some policy or measure is excluded on grounds that it will adversely affect an indefinite group of people.

Again, the public interest, in either its positive or negative applications, is not the will of all. Individuals may choose as members of the public, but they need not do so. Indeed, there is scant reason for liberal democrats either to expect that they will or to hold that they ought. Where decisions are made collectively, majority rule voting (or whatever other voting procedure is

---

*Intuitively, where all individuals agree, the social choice will be just that ordering on which there is unanimity. It is easy to show, formally, that a modified condition on Collective Rationality, according to which any input is admissible, so long as all inputs are the same (unanimity), is consistent with the remaining conditions, or, in other words, that a unanimity social welfare function is "possible."

deemed appropriate) combines individual choices whatever they are—not just those choices that bear on the public interest. In general, then, claims about the public interest are claims about hypothetical voting situations; about what *would* be the outcome of a vote *if*, as is contrary to what liberal democrats suppose, individuals voted *only* as members of the public. To claim that a measure or policy is in or contrary to the public interest, then, is to speculate about the outcome of a vote that, for the liberal democrat, would never take place.

Such speculation is plainly prone to abuse. We are asked, in effect, to engage in a thought experiment, the results of which cannot be checked by experience, and in which particular interests are very likely to intrude. This is why, as even the most ardent liberal democratic defenders of the concept must admit, group pressures of various sorts, sometimes only dimly concealed, motivate many, if not most, actual appeals to the public interest in ongoing liberal democracies. It may even be the case that existing liberal democratic polities, whatever their theoretical claims about the rational bases for cooperation among the individuals who constitute these political communities, are in fact so divided that any consensus on ends, no matter how hypothetical, is elusive. Then there would be, in fact, few if any policies or measures actually in the public interest (in the want-regarding, liberal democratic sense). But even so, to the extent that the aggregation problem is solved (or overlooked), the concept has a clear and intelligible meaning within liberal democratic theory.

For a measure or policy to be in the public interest, it must be the (hypothetical) choice of individuals voting, as it were, in their public personalities. Where there are shared common interests among individuals (as members of the public), the concept is entirely unproblematic. But the concept can and should be generalized beyond unanimity. Of course, where unanimity is lacking, the incoherence that plagues Arrow social welfare functions generally threatens to plague the public interest as well. Very likely, this difficulty does indeed affect the public interest, once the concept is generalized to encompass interests that are not commonly shared. However it might be that where all individuals assess alternatives as members of the public, their idiosyncratic differences will be vastly curtailed and, in consequence, their choices, while not always the same (unanimity), will be enough like one another to justify modifying the condition on Collective Rationality enough to admit only those inputs that satisfy structural properties sufficient for guaranteeing coherence. The problem in making the case for this speculation is that the significance of the many modifications of Collective Rationality that are formally sufficient for avoiding incoherence remain intractably difficult to interpret rigorously.[11] In any case, the generalized concept of the public interest is, at worst, no more problematic than the concept of democratic collective choice generally; and there is at least some reason to speculate that the concept is in fact viable.

Nonetheless, contrary to what many seem to want of the concept, the public interest, in the liberal democratic view, is hardly what political institutions exist to further. Indeed, there is very little that can be said within liberal democratic theory to support the widespread view that the public interest should be furthered at all. The contrast with idealism, where the realization of a very different sort of public interest is the essential burden of citizenship, could hardly be more pronounced. For that alternative tradition, citizens as citizens achieve a consensus on ends. As a citizen, one wills the public (general) interest. Public debate, then, has the character of "disinterested" deliberation, where what is in question is the relative merit of alternative ways to achieve agreed upon ends; public decision-making is, in effect, a pooling of these opinions. For the liberal democrat, however, to say that a measure or policy is in (or contrary to) the public interest is only to speculate on the outcome of a hypothetical collective choice. The public interest as such has no status different from any other collective choice. It in no way touches upon the nature or special duties of citizenship. It is neither more nor less than a collective decision arrived at (hypothetically) by individuals considering alternatives from a certain point of view.

And there is no particular reason to value that point of view, the point of view of members of the public, over any other point of view, including the most blatantly particular and self-seeking. Our substantive ends are beyond critical reproach. it is no more reasonable, or better, to be public-minded than to be self-seeking or altruistic or whatever. Our ends are whatever we take them to be, and no ideal-regarding valuation whatsoever attaches to them.

To be sure, as members of the public, individuals do want public interests furthered. And this task will very largely fall to the state. For if the public interest is not also the interest of some particular group, and if the state does not seek to further measures and policies in the public interest, then no one will. And if no one furthers the public interest, individuals will be worse off as members of the public—therefore, quite possibly, worse off *tout court*. Presumably, this is a consideration individuals will take into account in assessing alternatives for social choice. In general, there is a trade-off between the various points of view from which one assesses one's choices—in this case between public and other considerations. But this trade-off is determined, ultimately, by the "passions" (as Hume would have it) of each individual. Liberal democratic theory has nothing to say about how individuals ought to choose.

In sum, then, liberal democrats *can* argue that the state should further the public interest, but only, as it were, by default. The public interest is valuable only insofar as individuals regard it as such. It has no other—essential—connection to poiitical life. Therefore, the liberal democrat cannot say, as some might wish, that *the state exists to further the public interest*. Furthering the public interest may be a function of the state, if individuals so choose; but it is by no means the state's *raison d'être*.

We have seen that what underlies liberal democracy's uses

of interest is a view of practical reason as only instrumental, of reason as "the slave of the passion." It is this view too, as we saw in chapter 2, that underlies the liberal democrat's distinctive concept of freedom. It is, therefore, to this view of practical reason, the destination of this "regressive analysis" (Kant) of liberal democratic theory, that we now turn.

4 / Rational Agency

A theory of rational agency is an account of what it is to act rationally from the point of view of agents choosing among alternative courses of action. It is, I maintain, upon a particular notion of rational agency that what is conceptually distinctive in liberal democratic theory depends. This account of rational agency, then, is an account of the "foundations" of liberal democratic theory. The aim in this chapter is more to expose and describe these foundations than to critically evaluate them. From time to time, though, as in preceding chapters, it will be instructive to draw a contrast with the idealist tradition in political thought; this contrast will generally not be to liberal democracy's advantage. It is therefore worth repeating that my intent is not at all to endorse political idealism. Rather it is to emphasize what is distinctive— and vulnerable—in liberal democratic theory.

Liberal democracy's presupposed notion of rational agency is, we shall see, quite problematic. In stressing its particularity and also its affinities to the kind of society that produces and sustains liberal democracy, some of its more troublesome aspects will be brought into focus. But no full-fledged critical assault on this view of rational agency will be attempted here or in ensuing chapters. Throughout Part I, my concern is mainly to reconstruct liberal democratic theory as a genre of political argument and to bring its foundations to light, in preparation for a rather different kind of critical approach to be undertaken in Parts II and III. Thus whatever is intimated here against liberal democracy's presupposed notion of rational agency, as previously against its views of freedom and individuals' interests, is said, as it were, indirectly and in passing, in the course of attempting to specify, as perspicuously as possible, what liberal democratic theory is.

Ends and Means

Were the ends persons seek to realize such that they could be judged rational or irrational according to their content, as the idealist tradition supposes, and not just according to the formal relations pertaining between them, as is presupposed by liberal democracy's notion of freedom (see chapter 2) and of democratic collective choice (see chapter 1 and 3), a theory of rational agency and an account of human agency, of how human beings do or can act, might diverge radically. A theory of "pure practical reason," as Kant insisted, is methodologically non-anthropological; it must not depend in any way upon an account of how human beings are or might become, nor indeed upon any claims about "human nature." The categorical imperative, which for Kant rules on the content of our ends, is binding on rational agents as such. Whether human beings are already, or are capable of becoming, rational agents is of course a crucially important question for Kantian moral philosophy, but this is not a question germane to an account of rational agency itself.

The situation is quite otherwise, however, where, as in liberal democratic theory, practical reason is understood to be simply instrumental, and therefore to be indifferent to the content of the ends persons will. In this view, there can be no theory of pure practical reason, no account of rational agency independent of human agency. Indeed, the idealist vision of a rational world order, of a structure of ends enjoined by reason as such, is unthinkable for the liberal democrat. There is no rational order of ends—only the choices of actual men and women. These choices may, of course, be irrational in the senses discussed in chapter 2; they may be imprudent or, worse, inconsistent. But except for being *not irrational* in these senses, the liberal democrat, unlike the idealist, has no notion of rational ends. For, again, there is no rational order to which choices may or may not conform, and against which the choices of actual human beings may be critically assessed.

We have already seen how where practical reason is held to be only instrumental, rational behavior is viewed as maximizing behavior, as efficiency in the adaption of means to ends. To view rational agency this way, as remarked in chapter 2, is to suppose that a person's ends can be ordered according to his degree of preference (and indifference) for their realization. Traditionally it is thought that, at least in principle, this ordering can be represented quantitatively, where the measure of preference and indifference is called *utility*. Thus rational agents are utility maximizers. However, as we have seen for the theory of democratic collective choice, it is neither necessary nor always desirable for those who subscribe to this notion of rational agency to be strictly utilitarian, to suppose that utility can be measured and added. At least in political contexts, liberal democrats believe they realize the aggregative maximum by counting votes, not by adding utilities. The description of rational agents as utility maximizers should not, therefore, be understood literally. Liberal democracy's commitment is to a view of rational behavior as maximizing behavior, not to strict utilitarianism.

What one does, then, as a rational agent, as a utility maximizer, depends entirely upon matters of fact external to the theory of rational agency: upon the agent's values (represented by his ordering of the alternatives in contention), upon what these choices actually are, and upon the likelihood of realizing these choices (that is, upon their probability distributions). All that can be claimed on the basis of a theory of rational agency (of the liberal democratic sort) is that given one's values and given the concrete situation, the rational (human) agent will seek to do as well for himself as he can in the circumstances; that is, to realize for himself as much utility (understood loosely) as he can.

Given this account of what it is for an agent to act rationally, it is not hard to see how liberal democracy's distinctive notions of freedom and interest follow. Since virtually all elements of the rationale have been set out already in the two preceding chapters, it will suffice here to draw these elements together briefly and schematically.

It is because, in the liberal democratic view, there are no rational ends logically independent of persons' wants that liberal democrats effectively maintain the unthinkability of freedom as rational self-determination ("automony" in Rousseau's or Kant's sense); and insist instead that freedom is the absence of coercive restraint. If a person is free when and insofar as he does what he wants, and if wants are ultimately non- or extra-rational and therefore beyond critical reproach (except in the innocuous senses discussed in chapter 2), we are never justified in ascribing ends to persons or in "forcing persons to be free" (by forcing them to realize these ascribed ends). Then freedom cannot be other than the absence of restraint in the pursuit of one's ends (wants). To fulfill our nature as reasonable beings, we must be left alone to pursue our ends by our own lights. Characteristically, however, liberal democrats do not depict freedom's value in quite this way. Rationality, viewed just as maximizng behavior, is no doubt insufficiently lofty and appealing to stand as an ultimate value. Freedom is valued, characteristically, for its own sake: as an end-in-itself that social and political institutions should seek to promote.

However, as we know, not all liberals all of the time value freedom for its own sake. Thus in On Liberty and less directly in The Principles of Political Economy, Mill contended that freedom is not, strictly, to be valued as and end-in-itself, but as a means for furthering human welfare (in some suitably broad and "progressive" sense). It is debatable whether Mill consistently abided by this view of freedom's role, but to the extent he did, and to the extent others have followed him, the link between freedom and rational agency is developed somewhat differently from what we have already seen. If society is a collection of (atomic) individuals, all seeking to do as well for themselves as they can, and if individuals' value systems are radically independent of one another (as the atomic individualist picture of society suggests), so that there is no reason to expect people to have the same or even similar value systems, what actually constitutes social welfare will depend entirely upon the value systems of the individuals who constitute society. Then, so far as possible, individuals should be left free to pursue their own ends. As the ultimate source of their ends, persons are in a privileged position to know what their true ends are. And as rational (consistent and prudent) agents, they are in general better situated than others, and certainly better situated than the governement, to act in their own best interests. Therefore if the point is to maximize social welfare by increasing individuals' welfare levels as much as possible, it is best to leave individuals unrestrained in the pursuit of their ends. Provided there is enough coordination to overcome the state of war (of which more presently), the likely result will be the greatest possible welfare.

As we have seen, aggregative considerations also motivate the liberal democrat's commitment to democratic collective choice. Here the argument is by now sufficiently familiar. In concocting political institutions, self-interested utility maximizers invest sovereignty in collective choice rules thought to further individuals' interests. Hence the commitment to specifically democratic collective choice, and particularly to simple majority rule voting (see chapter 1); a commitment we now know to be ill-founded. Of course, reason as maximization does not by itself entail a commitment to democratic choice. Particular views of human nature and society also play a role, as we have seen. But an identification of rational behavior and maximizing behavior is a central element of the liberal democratic case for the democratic component. Were rational agency conceived differently, the liberal democrat's rationale for democracy would be undone at the root.

Again, it is not democratic collective choice as such that presupposes reason as maximization, but democratic choice for the sake of furthering individuals' (private) interests. Where rational behavior and maximizing behavior are not identified, as in the idealist tradition, there can still be a commitment to democratic collective choice, as Rousseau's example illustrates. But then the commitment is not to democracy as a means for achieving the aggregative maximum, but, as for Rousseau, for discovering the general interest—that is, for discovering what reason requires. Idealists can be democrats, but not liberal democrats; that is, not exponents of that type of democratic theory that in fusion with liberalism forms liberal democratic theory.

Hobbes' Argument

Focus on this view of rational human agency as (utility) maximizing facilitates a further restatement of the argument for sovereignty, sketched, following Hobbes, in chapter 1, and fairly, though anachronistically, ascribed to liberal democratic theory. The claim, in brief, is that unconstrained individual utility maximizing—as in society without the state, is a "state of nature"— does not always yield the best outcome for individual maximizers. Therefore it is in each person's interest to put maximizing behaviour (their own and others') under suitable constraints. In Hobbes' view, as we know, the institution of sovereignty establishes the proper constraints. The liberal democrat differs from Hobbes only in his view of the form and limits of the sovereign power. For present purposes, these differences are immaterial.

The difficulty with unconstrained utility maximizing arises in the context of interdependent action, where there are several rational agents, and where the outcome of an agent's choices depends, in part, on what other agents do.[1] The each rational agent must take each other agent's rationality into account in assessing alternative choices. An agent chooses on the assumption that others seek, correctly, to maximize their own expected utility, and that one's own rationality is taken into account by others, just as one takes others' rationality into account oneself.

It is of course not possible in general for all agents to achieve the best possible outcomes (for themselves)—particularly in the context of interdependent action. In general, individuals will fare differently, according to their utility functions, in different situations. If a situation is *best* only if it allows each agent to do at least as well for himself as in every other alternative situation, then, in nearly all cases, there is no best outcome. Accordingly, it would be vain and futile to suppose that, by choosing well, we can bring about best outcomes. However it can be shown that in every situation there must be at least one, and there may indeed be many, outcomes that accord each agent a maximum *compossible* utility— that is, where each agent receives as much utility as possible, given the utilities received by others. These outcomes are said by economists to be *efficient* or, more generally, *optimal*. Outcomes are optimal, then, when there is no other outcome according some agents more utility, that does not also accord others less.* It is surely reasonable, for adherents of the liberal democrat's view of interest (and thus a rational agency), to require that in every situation, each rational agent should seek to bring about an optimal outcome. For if the outcome is not optimal, there are alternative outcomes preferable on aggregative grounds, in the sense that some individuals would do better in these alternative outcomes, while no one would do worse.† But optimal outcomes are just what unconstrained individual utility maximizing cannot guarantee.

This situation is illustrated by the well-know Prisoner's Dilemma, which, taken as a counter-example, is sufficient for showing that unconstrainted utility maximizing will not always produce optimal outcomes. Suppose two prisoners are held, say, for armed robbery and also for resisting arrest. The prosecuting attorney has sufficient evidence for conviction for the latter charge, but cannot convict for armed robbery without a confession. He

---

*This notion of efficiency or optimality was formulated by Wilfredo Pareto and is designated, consequently, *Pareto optimality*.

†This conclusion presupposes that individuals are not envious or, more generally, that they are concerned only with payoffs to themselves, and therefore with payoffs to others only insofar as it affects payoffs to themselves. In other words, individuals are thought to be, in the current jargon, "non-tuistic," to take no interest in each others' interests. This very unrealistic assumption is virtually a dogma of the Hobbesian view of practical reason. Were it abandoned, most of the analytic apparatus of post-Hobbism, such as the notion of Pareto optimality, would fall by the way or, at best, be severely complicated.

therefore undertakes the following strategy. Separating the prisoners from one another, so that communication between them becomes impossible, he offers each the following deal. If one confesses and the other does not, the one who confesses can go free, while the accomplice will have to serve ten years in prison. If both confess, each will get, say, eight years in prison. And if neither confesses, since there is only evidence for conviction for resisting arrest, each will have to serve only one year in prison. If A and B are the two prisoners, these payoffs can be represented according to the matrix in figure 4.1, where the left-hand number of the pair of numbers represents years in prison for A, and the right-hand number represents years in prison for B. If A is a rational utility maximizer, he will reason as follows. The payoff for me depends on how B chooses. Either B will confess or he will not. If he confesses, then I had better confess as well, since the payoff for me will then be somewhat less bad (eight years in prison as opposed to ten). On the other hand, if B chooses not to confess, then certainly I should confess, since the payoff for me will be much better (freedom as opposed to a year in prison). Therefore, A decides to confess. Since the payoffs are exactly the same for B, given A's choices, and since B and A are equally rational utility maximizers, B too will decide to confess. Then each will confess and, in consequence, get eight-year prison sentences. But plainly this is not the optimal outcome. Each would do better (and therefore no one would do worse) if neither confessed. Namely $(-1,-1)$, not $(-8,-8)$ is the optimal solution, but $(-8,-8)$ is the outcome for independent, unconstrained maximizers. By choosing rationally, given their interests, A and B have failed to attain the optimal outcome.

If each of the two prisoners could trust the other *not* to act

	B confesses	B doesn't confess
A confesses	$-8, -8$	$0, -10$
A doesn't confess	$-10,\ \ 0$	$-1, -1$

Figure 4.1

as an individual utility maximizer, they would be able to achieve the optimal outcome. Neither prisoner would confess; each would receive only one year in prison, rather than eight. But there is no (rational) ground for trust. To attain the optimal outcome, each agent would, in effect, have to act irrationally. But why should a rational agent act irrationally? If one does and the other does not, then, according to the specified payoffs, the one who acts irrationally fares far worse than the other. It would therefore be unreasonable for either prisoner to decide unilaterally, as it were, to act irrationally. An enforceable agreement for each to act irrationally would, of course, solve the problem. In the case just sketched, to make their plight graphic, I stipulated that the prisoners cannot communicate. Thus an agreement between them is virtually impossible. But even if communication were allowed, can they coordinate their behavior sufficiently to achieve the optimal outcome?

By hypothesis, a rational agreement cannot require any person to perform an action which does not lead to an expected outcome with utility for him at least as great as the utility of the expected outcome for some alternative action. Therefore, self-interested rational agents, though they stand to benefit by agreeing (not to confess) are in effect obliged, so far as they are rational, to violate the terms of their agreement. There is, paradoxically, an inexorable motive to disobey the agreement, even though it is mutually advantageous. To abide by the agreement requires trust, and trust, in the situation depicted, is unreasonable. Individual utility maximizers cannot, therefore, reasonably coordinate their behavior in Prisoner's Dilemma situations so as to achieve optimal outcomes. This is why Hobbesians—and all liberal democrats are Hobbesians to this extent—cannot be anarchists. An internally coordinated association of rational agents, a society where cooperation is based exclusively on mutual (advantageous) agreements, is unworkable because it is not in general in the interest of rational agents intent on achieving optimal outcomes. Or, in other words, agreement alone is insufficient for organizing mutually advantageous cooperation in all cases. To do as well for

ourselves as we can, we need some form of *external (coercive)
coordination* that will constrain individuals' pursuit of their own
interests. We need to place ourselves in situations where we *cannot* always act as rational agents would in the context of *independent* action. In our interest, we need to constrain ourselves in
the pursuit of our interests.

But this is, as we have encountered it before, just the Hobbesian argument for sovereignty. We cannot escape the state of nature
by agreement alone. Only the external coordination of behavior,
guaranteed by an all-powerful sovereign, will save us from "the
war of all against all," the state of unconstrained individual maximizing. In the context of interdependent action, where political
institutions are possible, sovereignty becomes necessary. The state
of nature (which, for Hobbes, is a state of war) can thus be seen
as an n-person Prisoner's dilemma situation, for which the establishment of sovereignty, of implacable external coordination of
behavior, is the only viable solution. Sovereignty, for Hobbes and
also for the liberal democrat, is necessary for achieving optimal
outcomes.*

The inadequacy of straightforward individual utility maximizing, illustrated by the Prisoner's Dilemma, in no way impugns
the identification of rationality and maximization. Quite the contrary. It is because it fails in general to achieve optimal outcomes,
because it fails to maximize satisfactorily, that individual utility
maximizing is inadequate. Following Hobbes, liberal democrats
opt for states, and thereby for constraints on individual maximizing, *in the interest of individual maximizers.* They realize, at least
implicitly, that in the political sphere the "invisible hand" of the
classical economist, that promotes social welfare "unconsciously"

---

*For the liberal democrat, sovereignty is plainly not *sufficient* for achieving optimal
outcomes, however. As we have seen, to achieve the optimum, the liberal democrat
insists that sovereignty be invested in the entire people, assembled as a legislature,
voting according to the method of majority rule (or its close approximations). For
Hobbes too, sovereignty is likely not thought sufficient for achieving optimal outcomes. But, for reasons already considered (in chapter 1), Hobbes does not pursue
the quest for the optimum.

as individuals go about intentionally promoting their own interests, is not always at work. Rational agents, therefore, cannot always count on the invisible hand, but must supplement it, as it were, with the iron hand of the sovereign.

The mutual agreement to establish a framework of constraints on individual maximizing or, what effectively comes to the same thing, to establish states, is the hallmark of the *contractarian* tradition in political theory. Historically, however, liberal democrats have tended to distance themselves from that tradition, in favor of a more direct and sometimes explicit allegiance to utilitarianism (as Mill's own example illustrates perfectly) or sometimes to theories of individuals' rights.* Since this characteristic stance of liberal democrats is at variance with the rationale for liberal democratic theory, reconstructed in chapter 1 and resumed here, according to which liberal democracy's "grand theory" does rest on contractarian foundations, somethng must be said to account for this discrepancy.

The early development of contractarianism and the tendency of nineteenth-century scholarship to emphasize concrete historical investigation and accuracy, account in large part for the hostility of early liberal democrats, such as Mill and his contemporaries, toward contractarian political philosophy. It had been commonplace within the contractarian tradition to confound the historical problem of the *origin* pf political communities with the normative problem of the *foundation* (in right) of the state. Contractarian thought declined in the nineteenth century largely thanks to the increasingly evident untenability of the historical claim that existing states were founded by contract. Indeed, by the 1860s and 1870s, after Henry Sumner Maine had published his magisterial and influential study of *Ancient Law* (1861), it because accepted doctrine that the very idea of a contract, as a juridically binding agreement among distinct consenting parties,

---

*Contractarianism, utilitarianism, and appeals to individuals' rights need not be mutually exclusive. In fact, the literature abounds with examples of mixed forms. The most prominent mixed case is surely Locke's contractarian rights theory developed in the *Second Treatise on Government*.

emerged only very late in the history of European civilization. It has not been until quite recently that the the radical distinction between the historical and normative questions has come to be generally understood, though the great contractarians of the seventeenth and eighteenth centuries surely understood this distinction in practice. From a contemporary perspective, the abundant evidence weakening the historical hypothesis has nothing whatsoever to do with the propriety of social contract theory in political philosophy. But this was not generally acknowledged at the time of the inception and consolidation of liberal democratic theory. Accordingly, liberal democrats, during liberal democracy's "classical" period particularly, but today as well, have often been reluctant to have anything to do with the social contract.

A more important reason perhaps for early liberal democracy's hostility towards contractarianism—a hostility that, again, carries over into contemporary discussion—is the failure of liberal democrats—throughout the entire history of liberal democratic theory—to confront squarely the fundamental questions of grand political theory. Whatever the express declarations of liberal democrats, the logic of their position—particularly their (Hobbesian) views of freedom, interest and rational agency—commit them to an essentially Hobbesian and therefore contractarian justification for the establishment of states. If this affiliation is not generally acknowledged, it is because fundamental questions are not generally confronted. Both utilitarianism and contractarianism, as well as pertinent rights theories, share the notion of reason as maximization.* But the contractarians, as it were, understand the implications of this conception better than do the others. For contractarians realize that in the social context relevant for political theory, the context of interdependent action, individuals' best interests are served when individuals maximize under constraints

---

*See chapter 7. Like contractarians, rights theorists, in effect, aim to constrain individual utility maximizing by holding that (some) rights claims take precedence over aggregative (welfare) considerations. But rights theorists agree with contractarians and utilitarians that individuals' interests are what count in assessing social arrangements; they agree also in taking social welfare as a value to be maximized.

of the sort the Hobbesian sovereign can, but agreement alone cannot, establish. If the liberal democrat does not explicitly acknowledge this realization, so much the worse for his express views. Liberal democratic theory, idealized and reconstructed as a grand political theory, requires this contractarian grounding, even if in its actual historical manifestations, liberal democracy ignores or even misconstrues its own foundations.

Individualism

A full elaboration of the Hobbesian (and liberal democratic) notion of rational agency would amount to an account of maximization under contraints of a sort necessary and sufficient for producing optimal outcomes. If it can be shown that, in general, constrained maximization in the context of interdependent action can always produce optimal outcomes, then a theory of rational agency along Hobbesian lines would be at least internally coherent.[2] So far as is now known, it cannot yet be said with complete assurance that the Hobbesian account will stand the test of internal coherence. But neither is there any good reason to think it will not. This is not the place to pursue this question, except to note that if an internally coherent theory of reason as maximization cannot, finally, be developed, the view of rational agency liberal democrats and other Hobbesians support, and all that rests upon it, cannot be sustained. What follows, however, will assume that a coherent theory of reason as maximization can be developed, and will go on to raise other sorts of doubts about its adequacy as a theory of rational agency.

    The Hobbesian view of practical reason is profoundly at odds with virtually all important rival accounts in the history of Western philosophy. The idealist tradition that has coexisted with the tradition (or traditions) inaugurated by Hobbes, supposes a quite different view, according to which reason does rule substantively on our ends, prescribing some and proscribing others. In its view of the autonomy of reason, of the self-legislation of rationally enjoined ends, and in its insistence that rational ends are determined negatively, in terms of beings (persons) to be respected, rather than positively, in terms of substantive goals to be achieved, idealism differs from some of its important rivals and precursors, from Plato, most importantly, and from the Thomists. But whatever the differences distinguishing idealism from other views of practical reason, all positions, except Hobbes', agree that reason is more than merely instrumental. However accustomed we may have become to the Hobbesian account, however much, as a presupposition of the dominant ideology, the view of reason as maximization has become part of our common sense, we should never lose sight of its extreme historical particularity, and its profound variance from virtually all other serious accounts of practical reason. Of course, the particularity of the Hobbesian position in itself has no bearing on its adequacy. It would hardly even be relevant to note here, were it not that the virtually unchallenged dominance of liberal democratic theory has rendered its presupposed view of rational agency so commonplace, so deeply entrenched, that an historical perspective becomes important for appreciating its extreme radicalness—and also for sensing its vulnerability. It is with this end in view that a signal characteristic of the Hobbesian view should be noted here: the extreme individualism it suggests.

The rational agent, on the Hobbesian account, so far as willing is concerned, is radically independent of other rational agents. The men and women of a Hobbesian world, and of liberal democracy's core theory, are radically alone. There is no "harmony of rational wills" (Kant), as in the idealist tradition, in virtue of which community is intrinsic to rational willing. The Hobbesian account is tendentially individualist in the view of society it presupposes and, at the same time, reinforces.

To be sure, no concept of rational agency, Hobbesian or otherwise, individuates. To say that it is rational for an agent to do x is to say that for anyone similarly circumstanced, it is rational to do x, regardless of any differences distinguishing one individual from another. But for Hobbes and his followers, individuals A and B are similarly circumstanced only if A and B each will the same end (in the same situation), and the ends A and B will (like the situations in which they find themselves) are entirely contingent. Individuals' ends, let us say, are radically *disjoint*. Therefore human society can only be a collection of *discrete* maximizers, radically independent of one another and of society as such—therefore not, as rational agents, in solidary association.

In chapter 2, a society lacking community, comprising just a collection of radically independent individuals, was described as *atomic individualist*. The name is apt insofar as the ultimate constituents of social reality, the atoms, are individuals, essentially independent of one another and of society, bearing only extrinsic relations to one another. If, as should be generally conceded, an atomic individualist picture of society is not a normatively adequate ideal of a good society, if only because *community* is a value any adequate normative theory would incorporate, then its connections with atomic individualism speak against the Hobbesian—and liberal democratic—view of rational agency. What precisely are these connections?

As already pointed out, where persons' ends are disjoint an atomic individualist picture of society is immediately suggested. However, strictly speaking, atomic individualism does not follow from the Hobbesian view of rational agency. Atomic individualism does not follow precisely because, where reason is exclusively instrumental, no constraints whatever are placed on the content of our ends. Utility maximizers (suitably constrained) might seek to realize ends that are altruistic or social. They might even value association or community—not just as means for realizing other (egoistic) ends through cooperation, but for their own sake.

But if this view of rational agency does not strictly entail atomic individualism, it certainly inclines toward it. There is, we know, no principle according to which ends are brought together into a common framework. More important, everything and everyone threatens to become merely instrumental, to be a means for the satisfaction of antecedently given and essentially private ends. But if atomic individualism is to be avoided and if community is to exist, persons cannot be merely instrumental for one another.

There must be *intrinsic* relations between persons, and not only *extrinsic* ones.

The difference I have in mind between intrinsic and extrinsic relations may be illustrated by reference to some familiar accounts of social relations. According to the story Marx tells in the 1844 *Manuscripts*,[3] capitalists need workers because, for reasons having to do with the technical or economic conditions of production, workers' labor is, as a matter of fact, irreplaceable. Thus workers figure in capitalists ends only contingently. Wherever, as is generally the case throughout the economy, there is no necessary connection between the process and product of labor, the capitalist values only the product (in its commodity form) and not the labor itself. For capitalists, then, workers' value is strictly instrumental. The workers are means only, indistinguishable, valuationally, from tools or machines. In this sense, relations between capitalists and workers are *extrinsic*; there is no community. On the other hand, if Hegel is to be believed,[4] masters require slaves, not just as means for fulfilling desires in which the slaves do not themselves figure essentially, but also, primarily, to realize the value of domination (lordship). The master seeks the realization of his dominance in the slave's consciousness, and for the satisfaction of this end, the slave is plainly essential. Thus masters and slaves are related *intrinsically*. The master needs the slave, but not merely as a means. He needs, as it were, the slave himself. Thus master and slave form a kind of community—though, to be sure, not a democratic one.

A sense of the intrinsic value of others is important for virtually all traditions in political thought, except the Hobbesian and thus the liberal democratic. Idealism is particularly sensitive to this point, insisting, as in Kant's formulation, on a radical distinction between things and persons—where things are mere instrumentalities, but persons are "ends in themselves." The functional equivalent of this Kantian distinction must be maintained, if the liberal democrat is to find a place for those social or communal values he deems normatively appropriate (assuming, of course, the will to avoid atomic individualism). But this distinction cannot be maintained, as it is by Kant and throughout the idealist tradition, by appeal to rational agency.

Within the Hobbesian framework, if persons are expected to adopt social or communal ends, if they are expected (valuationally) to distinguish persons from things, it can only be for reasons that are, ultimately, psychological, because human nature is thought to be sociable and to consist of appropriate moral sentiments. Historically, of course, political theorists within the Hobbesian tradition, emphatically including the classical liberal democrats and most of their successors, have tended to assume the contrary. It has become commonplace to deny essential sociability; while exponents of a basically Hobbesian theory of practical reason have, from time to time, expounded theories of moral sentiments, their views have had relatively little impact on the development of specifically *political* thought. In general, then, a society of (utility) maximizers is indeed seen to be a society of atomic individuals.

Thus while the ground has been prepared, atomic individualism insinuates itself, finally, through psychology. Liberalism seldom, if ever, addresses these issues directly. Instead, it draws tacitly on Hobbesian moral psychology, on a notion of transhistorical, acquisitive human nature. But, strictly speaking, it is not necessary to subscribe to Hobbesian psychology. A determining role could be assigned to the effects of social relations upon a largely plastic human nature. The prototype of this sort of account is Rousseau's quasi-anthropological "history" of the development of *amour propre* (Hobbesian rational egoism) out of a much more benign *amour de soi* (self-love) in the *Discourse on the Origin of Inequality Among Men*. For Rousseau, rational egoism and therefore atomic individualism are socially generated, thanks largely to the institution of private property. For the present purpose, it is not important how this view of human nature is motivated, since liberalism, characteristically, just takes it for granted. What is important to point out here is that it is this view of acquisitive, self-interested human nature, however derived or justified, that promotes an atomic individualist view of society. It is in virtue of this assumed character of human beings that persons are typically, if not exclusively, egoists, that everything, including other persons, is subordinated to the quest for appropriation, and that everything is viewed instrumentally.

It may be, for Hobbes and perhaps for many liberal democratic writers as well, that their view of human nature as acquisitive is the most deeply entrenched aspect of their political thought, and the view of rational agency as maximizing is subscribed to, more or less unconsciously, as a suitable complement to this view. Then the theory of rational agency that underlies liberal democratic theory, and accounts for its most distinctive features, itself follows from a particular, and doubtless historically relative, conception of human nature. But whatever accounts for this view of practical reason, it is plain that conceptually the notion of acquisitive human nature is detachable from it; it can be maintained without also maintaining a view of acquisitive human nature. Why one would want to maintain such a view of rational agency, while subscribing to a different view of human nature, is another matter.

In any case, we can now see that it is its view of human nature and society, rather than its theory of rational agency *per se*, that accounts for some of the more contentious aspects of liberal democratic theory and other forms of political argument following in the wake of Hobbes. Inasmuch as these issues are best considered in the context of determining the feasibility of a "revisionist liberalism" free from what is apparently most objectionable in liberal democratic theory but retaining conceptual continuity with the core theory, it will be best to defer discussion until Part III. By way of conclusion, then, it will suffice to indicate briefly two contentious features of liberal democratic theory, at least in its classical versions, that do *not* follow from its presupposed notion of rational agency.

The first of these contentious features has already been pointed out in chapter 2: the claim that one is rendered unfree only in virtue of the *deliberate* activity of others. Nothing in the Hobbesian conception of practical reason requires this claim, nor indeed, as we have already seen, does any other part of liberal democracy's core theory.

A second contentious feature, very evident in Hobbes and persisting throughout much of the liberal democratic literature is the view, identified by C.B. Macpherson and others,[5] that the pursuit of utility is never-ending, that satisfaction is, at best, an ideal of (instrumental) reason, a goal to be sought, but never, in the nature of things, to be attained. On the contrary, in any situation where the alternative outcomes in contention are fixed, there is always in principle a best possible outcome, a maximum possible utility. Should this maximum be attained, it is entirely plausible to suppose that a rational agent would desist, at least for a time, from further maximizing behavior; that he would be satisfied or, at least, satiated. To deny this speculation is, in effect, to suppose that persons have no upper bounds or limits to their utility functions. Then the best possible outcome in a given circumstance—the outcome yielding the greatest utility of any alternative in contention—will not produce satisfaction. For there will always be other outcomes, not actually in contention, that would yield higher utilities, and for which the rational agent, Faust-like, will always strive. Then a satisfaction model of rational agency would be inappropriate. But it is, apparently, realistic, while the view that persons' utility functions are unbounded is not. But, again, the commitment to unbounded utility functions does not follow from the Hobbesian theory of rational agency. It follows rather from psychological assumptions about human beings, from characteristic, but conceptually detachable, claims about human beings' acquisitive nature.* It seems, then, that a revisionist liberalism can accommodate a picture of human behavior that is

---

*The neoclassical economic notion of marginal utility facilitates formulation of this tradition view of human agency. If money is a universal medium of exchange, then the claim amounts to the assertion that increments of money never have negative utility for rational human agents; that is, that everyone always wants more of *something*. There is, of course, decreasing marginal utility for money increments, but presumably this fact about individuals' preferences and indifferences is a consequence of trade-offs (for leisure or whatever) that arise in in the process of continuous acquisition.

richer and more congenial than that which liberal democratic theory, in its classical versions particularly but persisting to the present as well, has advanced.

These remarks, while not leaving the Hobbesian view of rational agency unscathed, by no means amount to a substantial assault upon it. My intent has been only to suggest its extreme historical particularity, and to intimate its vulnerability. Ultimately, this view of practical reason stands or falls less on its own right than with what is build upon it.

The view of reason as maximization is the end-point of this "regressive analysis" of liberal democratic theory. That analysis is only the first step in the task of critical evaluation. What follows are some further steps in that larger task.

Part II / The Joining of Liberalism and Democracy

THE guiding thread throughout Part II will be the question of the coherence of the liberal democratic project: the joining of liberalism and democracy into a single political theory. I will argue that the desired coherence is deeply problematic and very likely unattainable, and that liberal democracy's characteristic "solution" to the problem is won, as it were, at the democratic component's expense.

In making the case for this view, I will dwell on a number of related themes, each important in its own right for the critique of liberal democratic theory. The problem of joining liberalism and democracy will be posed in chapter 5. Chapter 6 considers Mill's efforts at a solution, and chapter 7 examines an alternative strategy, utilizing the concept of rights. The role of rights will be considered not only for the problem at hand, but also in the broader context of the liberal democrat's use of that concept. Then in chapter 8, in considering how liberal democrats effectively address the problems posed in chapter 5—scoring, in the end, a kind of Pyrrhic victory—I will remark on the philosophical importance of liberal democracy's use of political representation and its reliance on the institutions of representative government.

5 / The Liberal Democratic Project

AS presented in Part 1, liberal democratic theory is, in the first instance, an attempt to articulate, at the same time, both liberal and democratic judgments on political institutions. The liberal judgment, again, holds that there are aspects of an individual's life, including certain of his actions, which are private and with which others can never rightfully interfere.* The democratic judgment holds that what society does should be a function of each individual's choice for what society ought to do, where these choices are aggregated according to some "democratic" collective choice rule. Can these judgments coexist in a single, coherent political theory?

This question will seem odd to many contemporary liberal democrats for whom the coherence of liberal democratic theory is taken for granted. Once again, however, a historical perspective will underscore the pertinence of the question. If the first liberals were enemies of royal tyranny and the arbitrary uses of monarchical power, particularly where such power seemed to threaten property and its unimpeded accumulation, very early on "the tyranny of the majority"—a real historical possibility with the

*It is convenient, for now, to formulate this judgment in terms more congenial to Mill (see chapter 6) than to liberals who follow the strategy outlined in chapter 7. To allay confusion it should be noted that what is called "private" in this context need not coincide with what is called "private" in ordinary speech and even in the law. In general, the private sphere (in Mill's sense) will include many public (in the ordinary sense) acts, of the kind the U.S. Bill of Rights seeks to protect.

progressive extension of the democratic franchise—came to be seen as an even greater threat, at first to property accumulation and then to other areas of individual life that liberals sought to protect. Liberalism, then, developed in opposition to democracy, at least in its more radical applications. Thus it is far from obvious that liberalism and democracy can coesixt in a single, coherent political theory, whatever contemporary liberal democrats may suppose. My intent here is to explore the conceptual difficulties in the way of achieving this coherence.

I will argue that it is necessary to delineate the respective scopes of liberal self-determination and democratic collective choice. Among liberal democrats, John Stuart Mill is particularly clear in recognizing the need for scope delineation. The thesis of this chapter, then, is that Mill was right in this recognition: that liberal democratic theory must non-arbitrarily delineate the domains of the two components it seeks to join. Doing so is a condition for the viability of the liberal democratic project.

Paretian Liberalism

Recent work in the theory of collective choice, particularly A.K. Sen's demonstration of "the impossibility of a Paretian liberal," is of some pertinence in investigating what stands in the way of a coherent liberal democratic theory.[1] Sen's impossibility result reveals a rather unexpected conflict between liberalism and the notion of interest that motivates the democratic component. Recall that, for liberal democrats as for all Hobbesians, interests are reducible ultimately (though by no means directly) to wants. It is this notion of interest that motivates the liberal democrat's commitment to democratic collective choice: combining individuals' choices democratically is thought to be the way to maximize want-satisfaction as liberal democrats intend. A conflict between the liberal democratic notion of interest and liberalism is thus of some moment in ascertaining the requirements for joining liberalism and democracy. We shall see the the impossibility of Paretian liberalism, while not in itself devastating for the liberal democratic project, does underscore what appears to be an intractable conceptual problem for liberal democratic theory.

Sen reconstructs liberalism as a collective choice rule, as a principle for deriving social choices from individual choices for alternative possible outcomes. Needless to say, liberal democrats seldom, if ever, think of liberalism this way. But Sen's reconstruction is nonetheless entirely legitimate. To say that some aspects of an individual's life, and certain of his actions, are such that they can never rightfully be interfered with (coercively), is to say that with respect to *these* private choices, the individual is, so to speak, *sovereign*, and that the "collective choice" collapses, accordingly, into the individual's choice. That is, we assume that there is a fixed environment S of alternative outcomes in contention. If x and y are members of S, and if the choice between x and y is private for some individual i, the *liberal principle* (that is, the liberal value judgment, reconstructed as a collective choice rule), enjoins that i's choice with respect to x and y automatically be the social choice with respect to x and y.

Though appropriate, Sen's reconstruction is quite limited, and therefore by no means reconstructs the full "flesh and blood" of liberalism. A good deal of what traditional and contemporary liberals want to protect from societal and especially state interference is not captured by this rule. For the rule to apply, the choice between x and y must be private only for i. Consentual relations, then, do not fall under its scope; yet many consentual relations, whether in the marketplace or in more intimate quarters, are precisely the kinds of activities liberals seek to protect from societal interference. Nevertheless, this choice rule plainly does capture a necessary, though not a sufficient, characteristic of any liberal social philosophy.

Since the liberal principle applies only when alternative outcomes are private for some individual, most candidates for social choice fall outside its scope. For this reason, the liberal principle

will not do, by itself, as a collective choice rule for society.* At
best, it will be a part of a liberal polity's collective choice rule,
a value to be incorporated into a more inclusive constitution.

For a liberal *democrat*, collective choices are made by aggregating individuals' interests according to *democratic* choice procedures such as majority rule voting. We have seen how majority
rule voting and, more generally, any Arrow social welfare function
may not be capable of fulfilling its assigned function in democratic
theory; it may not be able to aggregate individuals' choices democratically. Bracketing these hesitations, however, and focusing
instead on the possibility of fusing democratic collective choice
and the liberal principle, even further difficulties can be brought
to light. Once again, Arrow's formulation of the problem is particularly helpful. Since the impossibility result in question here
depends on Arrow's formulation, it is worth briefly restating the
conditions that define an Arrow social welfare function. These
conditions, it will be recalled, are minimal, eminently reasonable
(if not beyond dispute), and mutually inconsistent.

Collective Rationality. For any logically possible individual
orderings, the collective choice rule determines an ordering
for the society.

Weak Pareto Principle. If one alternative is ranked higher
than another by all individuals, according to their orderings,
that alternative will rank higher in the social ordering.

Independence of Irrelevant Alternatives. For any set of alternative outcomes, the social choice depends only on the
individuals' orderings of the alternatives in contention.

Non-Dictatorship. There is no individual whose choices are

*We have seen in chapter 1 that a global liberalism, where all social choices fall
under the liberal principle, is unthinkable; such a liberalism is, in effect, a state
of nature (of a sort that liberal democrats, like all followers of Hobbes, have every
reason to avoid). Liberalism presupposes that there be political association and
therefore that the individual not always have exclusive sovereignty over himself.

automatically society's choices, regardless of the choices of all other individuals.

Liberalism requires that an individual be decisive over at least some alternatives in contention—specifically, those which are deemed private. But to say that an individual's choices are ever automatically the society's choices is to violate the Non-Dictatorship condition. To avoid that immediate clash, Sen proposes to construe the liberal principle as follows:

Minimal Liberalism. At least two individuals should have their personal choices reflected in social choice over one pair of alternatives each.

This formulation does not, strictly conflict with Non-Dictatorship. Still, it does, minimally, capture the intuition behind the liberal principle: that with respect to "private" choices, the individual is "sovereign." Even so, it is far from clear that Minimal Liberalism is strong enough to be of much use in a rational reconstruction of distinctively liberal theoretical positions. It is simply too weak. Still, as Sen proves, even this very weak condition, which is surely necessary for any collective choice rule that counts as liberal (though it is by no means sufficient), is inconsistent with Collective Rationality and the Weak Pareto Principle.*

The impossibility of an Arrow social welfare function is manifest in contradictory social choices or equivalently, as in the voting paradox, cyclical majorities. In this case too, the incoherence is manifest in cyclical majorities. Suppose there is some question—say, whether or not an individual should participate in a religious ceremony—for which the liberal principle is intended to be relevant. A person's decision on participation is surely "private," and, according to the liberal principle, should auto-

---

*Strictly, what Sen proves does not depend on the stipulation that the society have a transitive ordering of the alternatives in contention (as Collective Rationality requires), but only that the ordering be "acyclical", that if a is preferred to b, and b to c, and so on up to n, then n is not prefered to a. Transitivity would require that a be prefered to n.

matically become the social choice. Suppose there are two voters, A and B, who must decide whether: (w) A participates, (x) B participates, (y) A does not participate, and (z) B does not participate. Suppose further that A abhors religious ceremonies, and feels that, if either must participate, it is better that it be he, since B is susceptible to religious beliefs that A thinks harmful. Accordingly, A prefers z to y, y to w, w to x, and therefore z to x. B, on the other hand, approves of the ceremony and thinks it important that A be exposed to it. Accordingly, he prefers w to x, x to z, z to y, and therefore w to y. Presumably, liberalism requires that A's preference for y over w be the social choice (since the choice between w and y is private for A); and likewise, that B's choice of x over z be the social choice (since the choice between x and z is private for B). Thus the social choice must be such that y is preferred to w and x is preferred to z. By the Weak Pareto Principle, the society also chooses z over y, since z is higher in both A's and B's orderings than y is. But if x is chosen over z, and z over y, then x must also be chosen over w. However, by the Weak Pareto Principle, w is chosen over x. In other words, the joint operation of these conditions has given rise to a contradictory social choice, to a cyclical majority.

Note that Minimal Liberalism conflicts with what is least controversial in Arrow's formulation. In no way does it depend on the Independence of Irrelevant Alternatives. The Weak Pareto Principle is surely indispensible for any rational reconstruction of majority-rule voting or, indeed, for any democratic collective choice rule. The only chance, then, for integrating liberalism (even Minimal Liberalism) into a society's constitution alongside any democratic collective choice rule is to modify or abandon Collective Rationality.

As remarked in chapter 3, Collective Rationality is, in fact, an amalgam of two distinct claims: that the society have a transitive (or, at least, not cyclical) ordering of the alternatives in contention, and that the individual voters whose choices are to be combined may order the alternatives in any way they please (so long as they do so consistently). To abandon the first of these claims is not to solve the problem, but to decide (without good reason) to overlook it. Of course, there is no conflict between the Weak Pareto Principle and Minimal Liberalism over any particular pair or alternatives. However, it is not enough to have a collective choice rule capable of selecting alternatives presented pairwise. The point is to be capable of combining *orderings*. For reasons discussed already (in chapter 3), to require less is, in effect, to abandon the liberal democratic rationale for democratic collective choice.

All that remains, then, is to impose restrictions on individual orderings, to drop the stipulation that the choice mechanism produce an ordering from any logically possible input. As we have seen, there exists a substantial literature devoted to exploring this strategy, formulating necessary and sufficient conditions for ensuring (consistent) social orderings by imposing restrictions on inputs. In general, such restrictions are philosophically interesting to the extent that they reconstruct moves actually made in political arguments or anticipate moves that might be made. But, as we have seen (in chapter 3), *unrestricted* domain is a particularly apt requirement for liberal democratic society. Where the cultivation of individual differences (even if only in the "private" sphere) is a social goal and where individual values systems are radically independent of one another, there is every reason to suppose that idiosyncratic standards for evaluating alternatives will supersede any tendency for the universal adoption of common standards—of the sort that Collective Rationality with restricted domain might plausibly be thought to rationally reconstruct.

It seems, then, that there is no way out: Minimal Liberalism conflicts with the Weak Pareto Principle and Collective Rationality. The former cannot be abandoned, unless the goal of democratic collective choice is abandoned too. And, in all likelihood, neither can be the latter condition, at least in a way that will satisfactorily address the problem liberal democratic theory faces. Liberalism and democratic collective choice cannot coexist, it seems, in the same constitution.

Thus liberalism, even in the barely minimal sense recon-

structed by Sen, contradicts the liberal democrat's commitment
to aggregate individuals' interests (in the liberal democratic sense)
democratically. Can this difficulty be overcome?

Education

Plainly, the viable strategy is to render the demonstrated impossibility of Paretian liberalism benign, by effectively proscribing
cases where contradictions might arise. However such cases cannot even in principle be proscribed *constitutionally*, since to limit
individuals' choices in advance is inadmissibly undemocratic.
The impossibility of Paretian liberalism cannot, therefore, be legislated away. But it can be educated away.* In other words, to
maintain both liberalism (even Minimal Liberalism) and the Pareto
Principle, liberal democrats must attempt to arrange social institutions in such a way that individuals' value systems will be such
as to avoid patterns that give rise to Sen's impossibility result.
Citizens must be educated to liberal values. It is not enough, then,
to have liberal democratic constitutions. Liberal democratic polities require liberal democratic citizens.

Liberal democratic citizens, who value their own liberties
sufficiently, could always strike bargains insuring that their "private" choices (for which the liberal principle is intended to be
relevant) will be respected by others. In the case of participation
in the religious ceremony just described, A might negotiate with
B to the end that B would vote for *y* over *w*, contrary to B's given
preference; on condition that A vote for *x* over *z*, contrary to A's
given preference. Were such a bargain struck, both A's and B's
private choices would unequivocally be reflected in the social
choice. And such a bargain likely would be struck, so long as A
and B value their own liberty with sufficient intensity. If A and

---

Education here refers to whatever shapes individuals' values. In this sense, education is by no means confined to the schools, but is rather a function of all the
institutions of society.

B each value their own "free choices" more than their concerns with each other's behavior, it will be entirely in their respective interests to agree not to vote according to their given preferences, as described above, but instead to respect each others' private choices. And in doing so, they will have effectively avoided Sen's result.

Better still, were citizens educated not just to value their own liberty sufficiently to avoid incoherences, but to what might be called *full liberal consciousness*, the sorts of value systems A and B exhibit in their orderings would never occur—thus obviating even the need to bargain. Fully liberal citizens would take no interest in each others' private choices, except, of course, to value the realization of these choices, whatever they might be. Full liberal consciousness, the mentality of fully liberal citizens, thus *solves* the problem of the impossibility of Paretian liberalism. That impossibility arises, in effect, because Paretian liberals are not liberal enough, because they retain illiberal preferences for each others' behaviors. Were such illiberal preferences educated away, Sen's problem would be resolved and, one might suppose, the coherence of the liberal democratic project established.

But this latter impression is mistaken. Education will, at least in principle, render the theoretical problem Sen exhibits practically benign. But it will not suffice for establishing the coherence of the liberal democratic project. For this "solution" depends on solving a prior problem: the problem of determining, as it were, the content of full liberal consciousness. What, after all, is the proper scope of liberal self-determination? In what sorts of things ought fully conscious liberal citizens to take no interest? The liberal democrat must have satisfactory answers to these questions, in order to know what citizens are to be educated *toward*.

The liberal democrat must therefore determine the proper scopes of liberalism and democratic choice, respectively. Doing so, as we have just seen, is a precondition for meeting the challenge posed by Sen, a challenge that, if unmet, would severely threaten the liberal democratic project. And doing so is crucial too for addressing the more familiar, if recently forgotten, liberal democratic requirement of protecting against "the tyranny of the majority." If the liberal and the democratic components are to be practically reconciled, and if liberalism is to be adequately protected from democracy, the liberal democrat must, first of all, clearly and non-arbitrarily, determine what the liberal component is.

As already noted, the need for scope delineation or, what comes to the same thing, for specifying the content of the liberal component, is anticipated by Mill's insistence that the majority be sovereign only over certain kinds of *public* issues; and that in the *private* sphere, where the majority cannot rightfully legislate, the social choice should remain a matter of individual prerogative. However we know now that there is a potential conflict not just between liberalism and majoritarianism, but between liberalism and any collective choice rule that counts as democratic (in the very minimal sense of satisfying Arrow's and Sen's Weak Pareto Principle). The problem, in effect, is to determine what social choices should not be made democratically, and then—to meet Sens' problem, and no doubt more importantly (at least in practical terms), to insure a well-functioning liberal and democratic society—to shape individuals' preferences accordingly.

Schematically, it must be shown, first, that the respective scopes of liberalism and democracy can be delineated non-arbitrarily, in a theoretically well-motivated way. In more traditional, Millean terms, the problem is to distinguish the private from the public, the self-regarding from the other-regarding, the sphere of absolutely proscribed intereference from the sphere of permissible interference. As we shall go on to see, characteristically, this task is undertaken in one of two ways: either directly, as was Mill's strategy in *On Liberty*, or else with recourse to the notion of (in-alienable) *rights* that others can never rightfully infringe. On the former strategy, it is very evident that one must also demonstrate that in the sphere marked off as private, individual prerogative, not democratic collective choice, should govern. Appeals to individuals' rights sometimes obscure the need for this second step. In any case, however, it is clear that for the liberal democrat, the first and most basic task is to mark off a private sphere or its functional equivalent in terms of rights. Unless this task is carried out successfully, the justification for non-interference with what is private, or for the non-infringement of individuals' rights, cannot even properly be formulated.

As will be shown, this fundamental task, despite the best efforts of so many liberal democrats, remains quite intractable; the private/public distinction or the well-motivated specification of individuals' rights remain elusive. Yet the liberal democrat cannot make do otherwise. If liberalism and democracy are not to undo one another, indeed (in view of Sen's result) if they are not to contradict one another, liberal democratic theory must satisfactorily address the problem of scope delineation. And if, as seems likely, the prospects for doing so are poor, then so too are the prospects for liberal democratic theory.

The precarious character of the liberal democratic project, once felt so acutely by both liberals and democrats, but now largely overlooked by liberal democrats, must again be acknowledged as a crucial problem for liberal democratic theory. I will go on to argue that liberal democratic theory so far has not, and very likely cannot, solve this problem.

C. B. Macpherson has suggested that it required the emergence of particular institutions—above all, of representative parliaments and the party system—to channel and diffuse the exercise of popular sovereignty, before liberalism and democracy could be properly joined.[2] After arguing in chapters 6 and 7 that liberal democratic theory does not in fact have a satisfactory solution to the problem posed in this chapter, I will, in chapter 8, attempt to corroborate and amplify Macpherson's suggestion by focusing on liberal democracy's use of representative government. I will argue that the characteristic allegiance of liberal democrats to the institutions of representative government amounts to more than just an effort to approximate the direct democratic rule enjoined by the ideal theory, in practical circumstances where direct democratic rule is impracticable. To some degree, no doubt, the allegiance to representative institutions, and the pervasive tendency to view representatives as independent legislators rather than mandated delegates, derives from the residual influence of earlier, non-democratic political theories. But, more importantly, it amounts to an attempt to solve the problem of scope delineation: the problem of *fusing* liberalism and democracy coherently. Liberal democracy's solution is practical, rather than theoretical and, I shall argue, apparent, rather than genuine. The liberal democrat effectively overlooks what Rousseau long ago saw clearly: that with representative institutions (of the parliamentary sort) popular sovereignty goes by the board. Its form may remain, but not its substance. I shall argue, in short, that the sacrifice of popular sovereignty is the price liberal democrats pay for implementing the liberal democratic project.

6 / Private and Public

SATISFACTORILY addressing the problem of scope delineation will not by itself vindicate liberal democratic theory. But a solution is plainly necessary for any further vindication. Whatever else defenders may want to say on liberal democracy's behalf, they must at least establish the viability of the liberal democratic project. Is there, then, a theoretically well-motivated way to delineate the proper domains of liberalism and democracy, respectively?

I have already suggested that in *On Liberty*, a founding text of classical liberal democracy, John Stuart Mill effectively acknowledges and confronts this problem. This chapter examines the Millean position on scope delineation; though to develop that position perspicuously, it will sometimes be necessary to depart from the details of Mill's formulations. I will argue that, in the final analysis, Mill's strategy does not work. But its failure is nonetheless instructive for underscoring the nature of the problem liberal democratic theory faces and the enormous, and very likely insurmountable, difficulties that stand in the way of a solution.

The Private Sphere

Following Bentham, who regarded talk of rights outside specifically legal contexts as "nonsense," Mill announces at the very outset of *On Liberty* his intention to "forego any advantage that could be derived from the idea of abstract right as a thing independent of utility" and his corresponding intention to regard the principle of utility (in some suitably "large" sense, "grounded on the permanent interests of man as a progressive being") as "the ultimate appeal on all ethical questions."[1] It is far from sure that Mill in fact remains faithful to his express intentions. But for the matter at hand, the problem of delineating the respective domains of liberalism and democracy, Mill does indeed eschew talk of "abstract right as a thing independent of utility." What Mill proposed instead is best grasped by way of a spatial metaphor. Mill sought to demarcate an *area*—of individual life and behavior, of experiences of private consciousness and of "self-regarding" actions—that is *private*, in the sense that what transpires within this space, just as within the walls of a lord's castle, is the legitimate business of no one on the outside. Then whatever is not private, whatever occurs, so to speak, outside the walls of one's castle is *public*. Mill then went on to maintain that the private sphere ought to be immune from any form of state or societal (coercive) interference, while in the public sphere, democratic collective choice as well as other forms of interference may be allowable (in accordance with case by case utilitarian calculations). Even in the public sphere, Mill plainly maintained a presumption against interference, but in the private sphere, the ban is absolute and categorical. My concern here is not particularly to investigate this claim for the inviolability of the private sphere, but rather to examine what this claim presupposes: the division of individuals' lives and behaviors into private and public spheres.

It is often easy to discern where particular interferences fall for Mill and other liberals: whether in the private sphere (where they can never be legitimate) or in the public sphere. Thus Mill clearly regards questions of individual religious belief and practice (such as participation in the ceremony in question in the last chapter) and indeed most questions pertaining to the conduct of one's life as private; robbery and assault, as defined by existing legal arrangements, fall squarely in the public arena. There are gray areas, of course, even for Mill; a good deal of what has divided liberal writers has had to do with how particular gray cases should be sorted out. But the distinction is at least sufficiently clear for sorting some cases out unambiguously, and for providing a basis for reflecting upon the remaining gray areas. The question, then, is not whether the private/public distinction, as Mill wields it, is workable. For many purposes, it plainly is. Rather, the question is whether that distinction is tenable, whether it can be justified theoretically. Our intuitions alone, even if they were always clear, would not suffice. As Mill recognized, we need a *principle* for distinguishing the private from the public. We need such a principle not only to facilitate sorting cases out neatly and exhaustively. It is at least arguable that our intuitions, were they sufficiently clear, might do for that. We need a theoretically well-motivated principle because our intuitions about what is private and public, so far as they are themselves socially determined, are part of what is in question.

We need, in short, a critical vantage point for assessing the norms and practices of societies (including our own), regardless of the views (and intuitions) of the inhabitants of such societies. The principle that distinguishes the private from the public, then, should be specifiable apart from the norms and practices it is used to evaluate. Only a principle that stands, as it were, outside what is to be assessed will provide for the proper evaluation and criticism of a society's norms and practices, its laws and institutions, and even the intuitions of its members (as to what should and should not be others' business).

Lacking such a principle, prevailing norms and practices could of course still be critically assessed. The liberal can always appeal to intuitions, his own or what he takes to be those of (relevant) others, even if the warrant for doing so is unsubstantiated. Or the liberal might appeal to consistency. Thus if it is deemed acceptable that a particular book considered offensive by many in the community nonetheless be published and sold (say on grounds of "redeeming artistic or social importance"), then so too should other "offensive" books presently banned (provided they too have redeeming social or artistic importance). But for reasons already discussed (in chapter 1), liberalism requires more than such localized criticism; it requires an *a priori* specification of what counts as illegitimate interference. We must be able to *show*, regardless of people's views and therefore even if all disagree, that (to take an historically important, but quaintly outmoded example) *Lady Chatterley's Lover* ought not to be banned, no matter even if there is a consensus to the contrary. In other words, a principle that stands outside norms and ongoing practices is indispensable for the liberal project. Liberalism, it should not be forgotten, is a form of *radical* social criticism, for which all norms and practices, all institutions and laws, are subject to continual critical scrutiny.

Some indication of the elusiveness of the requisite critical vantage point may be gathered from even a cursory and superficial glance at the history of liberal "causes." Few, if any, issues of pertinence to social philosophy seem so entirely relativized, so profoundly dependent on historical and social circumstances, as the private/public distinction. The disposition of property, for example, was preeminently private for Locke and other early liberal writers, while today, many matters pertaining to property are thought to fall in the public sphere. On the other hand, the illegitimacy of "the enforcement of morals" has only lately come into its own as a liberal cause. There are, of course, some constant themes—religious liberty, freedom of the press, freedom of association—but even in these cases, doubtless, social change from the inception of liberalism to the present time has left its mark. It would be of considerable historical and theoretical interest to study the vicissitudes of the private/public distinction—that is, of what is taken to be private and public—within the liberal tradition. I think we could learn much from such a study about the complex relation between social philosophy and the society in which it is produced. But I would hazard we would find little guidance for producing a theoretically well-motivated private/public distinction, and further reason to doubt that such a distinction can be drawn.

Yet, as we have seen, liberal democratic theory cannot make do without such a distinction (or its functional equivalent)—as a precondition for any practical solution to "the impossibility of a Paretian liberal" and, above all, to save liberalism from democracy. It is misleading, then, to maintain, as some contemporary writers have suggested, that the liberal's concern is just to motivate grounds for (coercive) interference with individuals' freedom.[2] It is indeed true that insofar as freedom (in the Hobbesian sense) is a value, the presumption is always *against* interference; interference does require justification. But, as we have already seen (in chapter 1), liberalism requires more than a presumption against *all* interference; it requires categorical prohibition of certain types of interference. The liberal strain does tendentially enjoin minimal interference, but it is, definitively, a substantive theory, proscribing in advance interferences in specifiable domains. The reason for insisting on liberalism's substantive character is now evident. Substantive liberalism is liberalism with clearly defined boundaries, liberalism within a delineated domain. And domain delineation is crucial for the liberal democratic project.

The Harm Principle

It is to this end that we should understand Mill's celebrated account of the role of harm in justifying (coercive) interference. Mill advanced what may be called the *harm principle*: that the prevention of harm to others is a legitimate ground for coercive societal and state interference.* The rational intuition underlying this principle is, I think, a consequence of the core presupposition of formal liberalism: that each person be accorded the greatest freedom compatible with the cessation of a Hobbesian state of war or, what comes to the same thing, that political institutions, so far

---

*For Mill, the *others* in question are always specifiable individuals; thus harm to "the public" (some group on non-assignable individuals), insofar as such harm is not reducible to harm to specifiable others, is ruled out. Many contemporary liberals, however, relax this extreme, individualist understanding of harm, and countenance also harm to the public. Then it becomes possible to argue for coercive interference with activities thought to impair institutional practices or regulatory systems deemed to be in the public interest. On this distinction between "private" and "public" harm principles, see Feinberg, *Social Philosophy*, p. 25.

as possible, be minimal. It follows, then, that interference is always a harm-causing evil, albeit (so far as it is necessary to maintain a minimal state) a necessary one (to prevent the even greater evil of the state of war). For liberals, then, the harm principle is incontrovertible. But will it serve to establish substantive liberalism?

Recall that for Mill and many other liberals as well, the harm principle is deemed the *sole* legitimate ground for interfering with individuals' behavior. This claim for exclusivity is suggested, if not strictly entailed, by the foregoing considerations. Freedom is the value to be served, so far as possible, by political arrangements; the optimal level of freedom is achieved if all and only that (free) activity that impinges on others' (free) activity is proscribed. Any additional proscriptions, then, would move society away from the optimal level of freedom. Of course, even for the most orthodox liberals, values other than freedom might also motivate social policy. To the extent they do, the case for the exclusivity of the harm principle is weakened accordingly.

Mill, we know, claims to derive *all* considerations of social policy from a concern to maximize aggregate social welfare. This is, on the face of it, an implausible stance for the major theoretician of substantive liberalism. At the very least, it would seem that Mill's utilitarianism would lead him to support interference for the purpose of promoting social welfare. However, Mill plainly rejects interference for such ends. Moreover, he seems to defend the harm principle, and even to argue for its exclusivity, by appeal to welfare considerations. In other words, Mill argues that the principle which is his "ultimate appeal on all ethical questions"— that social policy be pursued exclusively according to welfare considerations ("in the largest sense, grounded on the permanent interests of man as a progressive being")—excludes interference to promote welfare, and allows interference only to serve a quite different end—preventing harm to others. Mill's is, in short, a very curious position, to which we shall return shortly.

Can we distinguish the private from the public by means of

the concept of harm? Mill's views on this question are not always clear, but at least sometimes he does seem to try to establish substantive liberalism this way.[3] The claim apparently, is that there are kinds of specifiable activities and practices that *in principle* are not harmful to others. These activities and practices constitute the private sphere where individual prerogative, not democratic collective choice, holds sway. Other activities and practices may be harmful to others, at least in principle. These constitute the public sphere. Private and public, then, are distinguished by reference to harm.

If this strategy for marking off the private sphere can be sustained, it would follow that Mill's theory of liberty does not, strictly, amount to an exclusive (and apparently problematic) commitment to the harm principle, but rather to a two-stage procedure for assessing specific interferences. This procedure, moreover, is entirely consonant with the spirit and letter of both formal and substantive liberalism. In assessing specific interferences, the first item to determine is whether the activity to be interfered with is private or public. This initial classification is accomplished by determining whether what is to be interfered with does or does not in principle harm others. If it does not, it is private and cannot be interfered with. (The rationale for prohibiting interference with what falls in the private sphere is sufficiently clear: since the activity in question does not in fact harm others, it having been determined that it cannot in principle do so, it would diminish aggregate welfare to interfere with the activity in question, since interference is itself an evil that diminishes aggregate welfare. There is, in short, nothing against which interference might be justified as the lesser evil).* If the activity in question is private, then, there is no need to inquire further. On the other hand, if the activity to be interfered with falls in the public sphere, we must inquire further to determine the relative (welfare) advantages of

*The obvious rejoinder, that the activity might be harmful to the perpetrator—indeed, sufficiently harmful to offset the evil of interference—thereby justifying interference on utilitarian grounds, is, as we shall see, acknowledged and dealt with by Mill.

coercive interference over a policy of benign neglect. Thus in the private sphere there is an absolute prohibition against coercive interference (as substantive liberalism requires), while in the public sphere there is a presumption against coercive interference (as formal liberalism requires), to be overruled only by compelling utilitarian considerations.

The Millean position, then, can be formulated as follows: that the specification of certain activities and practices that in principle are not harmful to others suffices to distinguish the private from the public and thereby to delimit the respective scopes of the liberal and democratic components. Whatever is picked out as private falls within the scope of individual prerogative, as liberalism intends. Whatever is public is susceptible to democratic collective choice or whatever other mechanisms of external coordination and control of individual behavior liberal democrats are prepared to allow.

To be sure, this reconstruction does not exhaust Mill's case for liberal democratic theory. It is, at most, a step along the way. If harm can be made to do the work Mill intends, and if social institutions are shaped accordingly, the coherence of the liberal democratic project will be at least formally guaranteed. However, as discussed in chapter 5, that coherence cannot finally be substantively guaranteed by constitutional means, but requires for its full realization, the education of the citizenry toward liberalism. This is indeed the principal political task for partisans of liberal democracy, even surpassing in importance the necessary consitutional struggles, as Mill clearly saw. We can constitutionally implement the requisite liberal restrictions on the scope of democratic collective choice, but we cannot, in the final anlaysis, legislate liberal democracy into existence. As with any momentous and sustained political vision, any ideal of good or proper political arrangements, the final battleground is in the field of "opinion" (to use the eighteenth-century term), and the stakes are ultimately the character of the individual's will.

Paternalism

However it is still not clear why, in Mill's view, if actions and practices harmful to *others* can be rightfully interfered with, actions harmful to *oneself* cannot. Actions harmful to others ought to be interfered with whenever the harm in question is great enough to offset the evil of interference. Surely similar considerations apply to harm to oneself. Interference to prevent harm to others is at least part of what is usually designated *paternalism*. What is the case against paternalism?

Even if a plausible case against full-blooded paternalism, against interference with a view to making persons better off, can be developed along the lines Mill advocated—by arguing that the likely outcomes of such interferences will not in general offset the evils of the interferences themselves—a limited paternalism, contrived just to prevent persons from harming themselves (as well as others), seems like it ought to be, from Mill's point of view, good social policy. Indeed, the case for limited paternalism seems to follow directly from Mill's commitment to utilitarian (welfare)calculations as "the ultimate appeal" in assessing social practices. As we know, Mill conceived of social welfare W_s as the summation of individual welfares $W_1, W_2, \ldots, W_n$, for individuals, $1, 2, \ldots n$. The point, then, is to maximize W_s. Then if an individual, say 1 would be better off for not squandering his small fortune—that is, if W_1 would be diminished by his doing so—and if the loss to 1 would not be off-set by welfare gains elsewhere (to other individuals), as is plausible in this example, then surely some social intervention is warranted on welfare grounds to prevent the decline in W_1 and consequently in W_s. And if such intervention, to be effective, requires coercive interference with 1's behavior, and not merely attempts at dissuasion, why shouldn't such interferences be permitted? This limited paternalism is not, it seems, affected by Mill's claim that paternalistic policies are generally counter-productive. Even if Mill is right in insisting that others cannot saitsfactorily ascertain what will promote our welfare (happiness) better than we can ourselves, so that societal interventions to promote welfare will be clumsy at best, and more frequently misdirected, we are nonetheless quite adept at identifying at least patent cases of foolish (non-maximizing) behavior and, at least sometimes, in seeing that persons engaging in such behavior would be better off (given their utilities) if prevented from engaging in it. Since social welfare is the sum of individual welfares, our concern to achieve the highest possible social welfare, W_s, should lead us, wherever possible, to prevent such foolishness, by whatever means are necessary.

Needless to say, Mill could hardly abide this result. For even limited paternalism would undo his carefully constructed substantive liberalism. Since virtually anything one does can in principle be harmful to oneself (if not, as Mill insists, to others), the class of categorically protected activities would shrink (if not quite to nothing, at least to nothing of consequence), and we would be left with no more than a presumption against interference—that is, with the formal liberalism Mill wanted, with good reason, to go beyond. It seems, in other words, that Mill's use of harm, whatever its advantages for delineating the liberal component, rests on arbitrarily restricting consideration to harm to others, when he ought to have appealed to harm in general (whether to others or to oneself), and that removing this restriction effectively undoes what Mill seems to have achieved in delineating the scope of the liberal component.

Mill is uncharacteristically indirect in denying that harm to oneself be a ground for restricting liberty. At the very outset of On Liberty, he states his thesis clearly and forthrightly—that the prevention of harm to others is the sole legitimate ground for coercive interference with individuals' actions. But then, in the course of denying alternative positions, he neglects to mention harm to oneself. His words bear repeating here, as much for their perspicuity, as for their omissions:

... the only purpose for which power can be rightfully exercised over any member of a civilized community, against his will, is to prevent harm to others. His own good, either physical or moral, is not a sufficient warrant. He cannot rightfully be compelled to do or forbear because it will be better for him to do so, because it will make him happier, because in the opinions of others, to do so would be wise or even right. These are good reasons for remonstrating with him, or reasoning with him, or persuading him, or entreating him, but not for compelling him, or visiting him with any evil in case he do otherwise. To justify that, the conduct from which it is desired to deter him must be calculated to produce evil in someone else . . . .[4]

One cannot, in Mill's view, rightfully interfere to promote someone's good, as full-blooded paternalism would have us do, and one can interfere to prevent harm to *others*. But the prevention of harm to oneself, limited paternalism, though implicitly denied (inasmuch as "the *only purpose* for which power can be rightfully exercised . . . is to prevent harm to others"), is never directly mentioned.

I would hazard that this omission, in a passage that is otherwise so forthright, is an implicit, and very likely unconscious, acknowledgment of the ultimately arbitrary character of excluding consideration of harm to oneself. Mill needs that exclusion, however, if the appeal to harm is to work to delineate the scope of the liberal component. But whatever makes the prevention of harm to others a plausible ground for allowing interference seems to hold as well for harm to oneself. Thus the exclusion of harm to oneself, however crucial for Mill's efforts to develop a substantive liberalism, apparently cannot be justified.

What Is Harm?

Even if Mill could justify the exclusion of paternalistic interference, will the appeal to harm (to others) in fact mark off the private from the public, as Mill intends? To come to terms with this question, we need to clarify what harm to others means. The tradition is sensitive to the difference between harm (in the relevant sense) and the infliction of some injury or hurt. One can be harmed without being (at least knowingly) hurt, as when, unbeknownst to the victim, some of his property is damaged or stolen.

And at least minor hurts and injuries are generally not thought to constitute harm. According to a widely held view, the object of harm, whether to specifiable individuals (as Mill would have it) or to "the public," is always an *interest*.[5] There is, however, an ambiguity in this use of interest that gives rise to an insurmountable difficulty. I will argue that this difficulty undoes Mill's best efforts to distinguish the private from the public by appeal to harm—even if the arbitrary restriction on which that attempt rests is conceded.

If "interest" is understood as liberal democrats are wont to (see chapter 3), they are reducible ultimately to wants. And inasmuch as wants are substantively unconstrained, so that anyone may want anything, interests, correspondingly, may be in anything, and therefore, as we saw in the last chapter, in activities that liberals want to protect from (coercive) societal and state interference. In short, where interest is understood as liberal democrats are accustomed to (and, indeed, obliged by the core theory), there is no reason in general to suppose that cases will be sorted out as liberals intend, and every reason to expect that virtually everything will fall in the public sphere (at least insofar as people are, as they might always be, illiberal in their wants). To remain faithful to the core notion of interest, some theoretically well-motivated adjustment will be necessary to sort cases out in the intended way. Somehow individuals' interests will have to be restricted appropriately, without passing over into ideal-regarding understandings of the notion. Otherwise the private/public distinction Mill wants and liberal democratic theory requires will remain elusive.

To the best of my knowledge, while dissatisfaction with Mill's use of harm is widespread, no one has satisfactorily corrected Mill by showing how troublesome, illiberal interests can be ruled out, and remained at the same time faithful to the liberal democratic sense of the term.[6] And I am doubtful anyone ever will. Liberal democrats, if not liberals generally, cannot legislate bothersome interests away, without doing violence to their democratic commitments (as reconstructed appropriately by Arrow's condition on Collective Rationality). For liberal democrats, attempts to legislate troublesome interests out of court will remain arbitrary finagling.

In fact, I think that very often, when interest is invoked as the object of harm, whether by Mill or by others, there is a tendency to understand that notion in an ideal-regarding sense that is, strictly, foreign to liberal democratic theory. An ideal-regarding notion of interest is, as it were, imported into liberal democratic theory *ad hoc* only for the purpose of motivating the private/public distinction. It is as an ideal-regarding notion, it seems, that we must understand the interests liberal writers, especially in legal contexts, allege in, among other things, personality, property, reputation, domestic relations, privacy or whatever.[7] These interests are claimed to exist independent of persons' wants. They are ascribed interests. The question, then, is whether there can be any theoretical warrant for making these interest ascriptions.

Idealist philosophy offers at least a basis for developing an answer. If we can give an account of the ends proper for rational agents or, as in Kantian moral philosophy, a theory of rational agency in its own right as an end-in-itself, then we might go on to determine the proper interests of humankind as those that encourage the realization of our proper ends.[8] We would then have a theory of *de jure*, and not merely *de facto*, interests, a theory independent of empirically acknowledged interests, purporting to establish what persons' "real" interests are. Liberal democratic theory, however, cannot support an ideal-regarding analysis of interest, even if it characteristically imports such a notion into its actual applications of the harm principle. This borrowing from idealism is *ad hoc*; an idealist notion of interest is effectively used, but not incorporated. Indeed, an idealist notion of interest can never be incorporated into liberal democratic theory. For to do so would be to deny what we have found (in chapter 4) to be liberal democracy's most fundamental theoretical presupposition: its notion of practical reason, according to which there are no ends proper for rational agents as such because reason does not rule over the content of our ends. Liberal democratic theory can hardly support a notion incompatible with its most fundamental presupposition. Idealism cannot save the Millean strategy.

It seems then that the only recourse is to appeal to prevailing norms as to what should count as private and public, in order to develop a suitably restrictive theory of interests. But of course this strategy is unsatisfactory. For prevailing norms are part of what the liberal principle is supposed to critically evaluate. Nonetheless, *faute de mieux*, it is just this strategy that liberals from Mill on have characteristically adopted. So far from discovering the requisite critical vantage point, they have thus fallen into a vicious circle, where socially produced norms supply the bases for their own critical evaluation.[9].

Mill's use of the harm principle to mark off the private from the public spheres thus encounters what seems to be an intractable dilemma wherever, as liberal democrats would have it, harm is understood as the invasion of persons' interests. If circularity is to be avoided, and if interest is construed in proper liberal democratic fashion, we cannot sort cases out into private and public spheres in anything like the intended way. On the other hand, if we import an idealist understanding of interest in order to draw the distinction as intended, we arbitrarily and eclectically transgress the frontiers of liberal democratic theory's underlying conceptual framework. There appears to be no way out of this dilemma, and no way to avoid it. Thus the appeal to harm, even if (arbitrarily) restricted to apply only to harm to others and not to oneself, will not do, finally, to mark off the private from the public.

In recent years, considerable effort has been spent attempting to clarify the complex connections between the concept of harm and related notions such as offense, hurt, non-benefit and so forth. In consequence, it may well be clearer now than it was for Mill what it *means* to harm another. But the liberal needs to know *when* activity is harmful, not just what it means for it to be so, and this determination must be made in a way that will do for constructing that critical vantage point from which everything of pertinence, including the norms and intuitions of the investigator, can be judged. To this end, I think, the investigations already undertaken and indeed any investigations likely to be undertaken along these lines will be of little, if any, use. For there appears to be no satisfactory way to do what liberalism requires.

Prospects After Mill

What liberalism requires (in the Millean formulation) is a non-arbitrary, theoretical determination of what ought to count as private. This determination can never be given, as it were, on the face of the actions and practices in question. Plainly, everything we do, even our most private and solitary occupations, can affect others somehow. No action, as Mill was entirely aware, is "self-regarding" in the sense that it (literally) affects only oneself. The very idea of an action affecting only oneself is, at best, a limiting-concept, to be approximated in some instances, but never, except perhaps in trivial cases, to be fully realized. It is for this reason that the Millean distinction between self-regarding and other-regarding actions (terms Mill himself never actually used) was always intended as a *valuational* distinction, not as a matter of fact. Mill indicated this intention in his labors to distinguish consequences of actions that *directly* affect the interests of others from those that do so only *indirectly* or *remotely*. Actions affect others directly only if they bear on (legitimate) interests these other persons hold; otherwise the effect is only indirect or remote. Then anything that invades an indirect interest does not count as harm. In Mill's terms, then, the problem is to give a theoretically well-motivated account of the difference between direct and indirect effects on interests. Until this is done, the valuational basis for the distinction between self-regarding and other-regarding actions, the main part of the distinction between the private and the public spheres, will always be arbitrary or, as I have suggested often happens in practice, circular. Mill's best efforts fail to avoid this unhappy result, even if, more than a century later, they remain liberal democracy's most sustained and important attempt at a solution.

The great merit of *On Liberty* is that it squarely poses and addresses the problem any liberal democratic theory must face for the liberal democratic project to succeed: the problem of limiting the respective scopes of its liberal and democratic components. Mill sought a non-arbitrary solution to this problem, and his efforts, I suspect, push as far as one can. Ultimately, however, these efforts fail. Mill does not satisfactorily resolve the problem he so perspicuously poses and so boldly confronts. Before we conclude, however, that this problem is insoluble, that the respective domains of the liberal and democratic components cannot be delineated non-arbitrarily, with all the consequences for the liberal democratic project that would follow, we must consider what, historically, is very likely the strategy most often used for achieving, among other things, the end Mill sought in vain: recourse to "the abstract concept of right, as a thing independent of utility." Once again, we should recall Mill's scorn for this strategy and his denunciation of it as theoretically arbitrary and without foundation.

7 / Rights

RIGHT is, by origin, a legal notion that, since the seventeenth century, has figured prominently throughout moral discourse. In its original sense, a right is a claim advanced by an individual or group, enforceable by law. Some prominent exceptions notwithstanding,* the concept has nearly always been understood normatively. To talk of rights is to talk of what the law *ought* to enforce, not of what it does in fact enforce. But, as a normative concept, it has long seemed unduly restrictive to limit talk of rights to particular juridical frameworks. And so, very early on, the concept of right outgrew its strictly legal sense. By *right*, then, is understood any legitimate claim advanced by an individual or group. In general, rights continue to be claimed within social frameworks. Rights are possessed in relation to others, and rights claims are directed, forensically, to these others. To talk of rights is to presuppose the existence of a community in which rights claims are advanced.

Even those who in the seventeenth or eighteenth centuries spoke of "natural" or "God-given" rights, and contemporary libertarians and others who have effectively taken over this view of rights as something individuals somehow *just have*, effectively understand, even if they do not always expressly acknowledge, the communal aspect of rights claims. John Locke's use of rights

---

*Among the most prominent exceptions are the legal realists, such as Jerome Frank and K.N. Llewellyn, for whom rights ascriptions are just predictions of what courts will do. However even those who construe legal rights this way still understand *moral rights* normatively.

is a case in point, and is particularly germane here inasmuch as Locke virtually inaugurated the specifically liberal use of the concept.[1] To say, as Locke does, that persons in the state of nature already have rights (because God has so bestowed them) is to say that, even in the state of nature, these rights ought to be acknowledged—and moreover will be acknowledged to the extent that God has given humankind the gift to discern them—even if they cannot yet be enforced. Locke's state of nature is not at all, as was Hobbes', a collection of individuals at war with one another. For Locke, the state of nature lacks only effective means for the enforcement of already acknowledged rights.* People have rights without the state, Locke tells us, "yet the enjoyment of [them] is very uncertain and constantly exposed to the invasion of others." It is to escape this "very unsafe, very insecure" condition that reasonable individuals contract together to establish a universal "umpire" with the power to enforce whatever rights claims are acknowledged.[2] These rights are God-given and, as it were, an individual's patrimony. But they are nonetheless in essence social: they are directed, forensically, to others. On Locke's account, rights claims are pre-political, but they are not, and cannot be, pre-social. For even if, as Locke thought, rights are not held in virtue of membership in a community (but are rather bestowed by God), they still presuppose *others* to whom they are addressed.

Likewise, those who today speak of *human rights*, the descendent, on some accounts, of Locke's natural rights,[3] speak of claims advanced within and addressed to "the human community." These rights are held, it is thought, by all humans, and are binding on all one's fellow human beings. For those who are at peace with the concept of right as such, the existence of human

*Two aspects of Locke's position should be noted here. First, for Locke, natural rights have to do overwhelmingly with the possession and disposition of property. It is in life, liberty *and property*, in Locke's view, that we have natural rights. Second, these rights are held to be "inalienable." Thus they cannot rightfully be transferred to the sovereign in a social contract. It is in this way that, in contractarian idiom, Locke effectively formulates the liberal principle. Whatever is not given up (alienated) remains under the sovereignty of the individual "holder" of these rights. And this sovereignty is then inviolable.

rights depends upon the cogency of conceiving a human community; the nature and extent of human rights depends upon the character of that community.[4] But whatever special problems there may be in the way of developing an adequate theory of human rights, those who would use the notion of right at all first must establish the viability of the concept as such, in its normative, extra-legal sense. This problem holds emphatically too for those who would use the concept of rights to restrict the scope of democratic collective choice and thus to meet the problems posed in chapter 5.

Talk of rights today has become so natural, so pervasive, that it is easy to lose sight of the need to justify the concept. Curiously, it is liberal democrats who have come to take the concept most ardently, despite Mill's repeated insistence that there is, in fact, no theoretically well-motivated way to assign rights to persons (other than by making utilitarian calculations, and then invoking the concept of right as a shorthand expression for the results of these calculations). If Mill is right, it could hardly make sense to talk of individuals "possessing" inalienable rights—that is, rights that cannot be given up for utilitarian reasons. Liberal democrats today must come to terms with this challenge laid down by liberal democratic theory's founding father. Either a viable theory of rights must be developed, or else the concept should be abandoned. And if the latter alternative proves inevitable, then plainly rights cannot be used, as Mill attempted to use the private/public distinction, to make the liberal democratic project coherent.

Doubtless this use of the concept of right is seldom, if ever, explicit in the liberal democratic literature; and, for all liberal democrats who "take rights seriously,"[5] the concept has uses that go beyond addressing the conceptual problem of constructing a coherent, liberal democratic theory. It is best, therefore, to focus on rights in this broader context. To this end, I shall explore some of the conceptual links between the concept of right, as it figures in liberal democratic discussions, and other elements of liberal democratic theory—particularly its notion of freedom. I will argue that talk of rights in general, and *a fortiori* of those rights liberals want to protect from societal and state interference—presupposes liberalism's particular view of freedom—the view that to be free is to be unrestrained by others in the pursuit of one's ends (see chapter 2). I will argue that within liberalism the concept of right plays a role that is, at once, crucial and arbitrary, and that, however, important for making liberalism attractive, in the end the concept will not serve to make liberal democratic theory coherent.

Liberal democrats' recourse to rights—in this broader context—is well worth reflecting upon. Doing so will bring to light both liberalism's good intentions and also its extreme theoretical vulnerability. I will therefore consider that not only those rights ascriptions that are specifically liberal in intent but the full range of so-called human rights sometimes advocated by liberal democrats (and, of course, by others as well). I will maintain that, for liberal democrats, the concept of human rights serves as a *corrective* within a politics that tends to fragment social solidarity while promoting an individualism that threatens what Kant calls "respect for persons." Within liberal democratic theory, the possession of human rights is the principal means for maintaining a sense of human dignity. This is why human rights, unlike other "possessions," cannot normally be traded off; why human rights are, in the traditional idiom, *inalienable*. To truck and barter in human rights is to detract from essential humanity, from human dignity, and to reduce persons to mere things. Of course, respect for persons and the radical distinction between persons and things can and has been theorized differently (see chapter 4). A good deal of idealist political theory is directed precisely to this end. But whatever the merits or defects of alternative accounts, liberal democracy generally supports respect for persons through the ascription of rights. And if rights ascriptions ultimately are arbitrary, this protection is fragile and not susceptible, apparently, of shoring up. Ultimately, one would expect that what liberal democrats articulate through recourse to rights is better conceived, and better defended, otherwise. However this is not the place to speculate on alternative strategies, whether those already extant (within the idealist tradition) or those that might be developed. It is enough for the present to probe the fragility of the dominant tradition.

Human Rights

Needless to say, there is scant consensus on what human rights persons "possess." It is therefore impossible to list human rights exhaustively or uncontroversially. However some generalization and even classification is in order. For convenience, then, let us group human rights into three relatively distinct categories.

Of greatest interest for this study are those putative human rights that aim to capture what Mill sought to locate in the private sphere, those rights that, we may still hope, will satisfactorily limit the scope of democratic collective choice. We have already seen how what is thought to fall within the private sphere varies considerably within the history of liberal democracy. This same historical variability carries over, of course, into rights ascriptions. Still, we can say roughly what falls within this category: the rights to free speech, to freedom of assembly, and to freedom of the press, the right to worship as one pleases (or not at all), the right to live as one wishes (at least in certain respects), and so on. Such rights imply a corresponding duty on the part of others, and particularly the state, not to interfere with individuals' behavior. In this way, as liberal democratic theory requires, the power of the state is limited by the rights of its citizens. We shall return to these liberal rights shortly.

Traditionally, such rights have not been ascribed to human beings as such, but only to persons thought capable of exercising them responsibly or for good ends. Thus Mill excluded children, idiots, lunatics and, as one might expect of a nineteenth-century Englishman, colonial peoples (or, at least, those that Europeans deemed "savages"). These categories of human beings were excluded because they were thought not to have developed the requisite moral and intellectual capacities for exercising liberty well. On the other hand, adult English men and women, in possession of their faculties, having come of age under liberal institutions, are deemed capable, as are those whose experience is similar. Such persons, accordingly, are to be protected from state and societal interference. Mill, of course, did not speak of rights in the sense under consideration here, but the point carries over for those who do. To the extent these exclusions are maintained, it is not quite correct to call the traditional liberties human rights, current usage notwithstanding, since there are human beings for whom they are not claimed. For now, however, it will be convenient to observe current usage with the implicit proviso that many of these rights, in their intended scope, are somewhat less than full human rights in the literal sense.

To these liberal rights are sometimes added certain specifically political rights: the right to vote, the right to fair treatment in courts of law, the right to travel, to emigrate, and so on. Plainly, these rights claims are advanced within specific institutional frameworks. It is as a citizen of X, that I claim the right to vote in X, or to fair treatment in its courts, or to a passport. If these rights are thought to be human rights, we may suppose that citizenship itself—indeed, citizenship in a political community of a sort that maintains these rights—is being claimed as a human right. Citizenship in this sense is not a liberty, a right to be left to do as one pleases, but a status incumbent with benefits and duties. Our human rights, falling under this category, would consist, then, of those benefits and duties that are thought proper for all persons, regardless of membership in particular communities. Presumably, those who would advance human rights claims of this sort would want to specify these rights minimally, as lowest common denominators of (acceptable) forms of citizenship. Thus the right to fair treatment in courts of law might count as a human right, while the right to "due process," in the sense of the U.S. Constitution, or the right to avoid self-incrimination, would more likely count as rights enjoyed in virtue of membership in particular polities. However, in all cases, the implementation and enforcement of these rights is a task, a "correlative obligation," of governments.

In recent decades, human rights claims of a still different sort have been advanced. Thus the Preamble to the United Nations' *Universal Declaration of Human Rights* (1948) announces that at least some of the rights that document claims as human rights should be construed as "a common standard of achievement for all peoples"; and this is generally taken to mean that these human rights articulate basic human needs (in the form of claims on others) without specifying correlative obligations on the part of governments (or anyone else, including international organizations) to implement these needs.[6] It is in this spirit, it is argued, that the U.N. *Declaration* announces human rights to "social security" (article 22), "to a standard of living adequate for health and well-being" of all persons "including food, clothing and housing" (article 25), and so on. Presumably, in declaring a human right, say, to clothing adequate for health and well-being, it is not being claimed that the government under which one lives has an obligation to supply clothing to its citizens (except perhaps in cases of extreme indigence or misfortune, where there is no other means for adequate clothing to be acquired). The sense of the claim, it seems, is that governments (and others as well) should seek to create conditions in which, other things being equal, its citizens may be adequately clothed. However this may be, it is significant that with the advent of such pronouncements about human rights, the range of the concept is extended—beyond liberties, beyond (minimal) rights of citizenship—to include at least minimal levels of social welfare. This extension underscores the role rights ascriptions play in implementing respect for persons.

What is shared by claims for non-interference with individuals' activities of the sort advanced by traditional liberalism, for citizenship with its attendant benefits and duties, and for a minimal level of social goods is precisely respect for persons, for human dignity as such. For these rights, exclusions apart, are claimed just in virtue of being human, and not in consequence of voluntary agreements or social arrangements of any sort. Our humanity, it seems, is bound up with the possession of these rights. Thus it is thought by most liberals (and, of course, by others as well) that human life cannot be fulfilled, that "powers" (in Hobbes' sense) cannot be developed, if liberty is unduly restricted.* So too it is thought by many that a fully human life cannot be achieved if citizenship is effectively denied, and if the availability of social goods is so reduced that life itself becomes nothing more than a struggle for survival. It is by articulating these claims forensically, by claiming rights to the conditions for being fully human, that respect for persons is asserted. Liberal democrats, if they make claims for human dignity at all, do so most naturally by ascribing rights to persons, and their persistence in claiming rights, and taking rights seriously, accounts for much that is attractive in the liberal democrat's view of social and political arrangements. But these rights claims, as we are now able to see, are made *against* what is implicit in liberal democracy's core notions of freedom and interest. Even if liberal democrats are not, strictly, inconsistent in advancing claims for rights of the sort considered here, for inalienable human rights, in doing so they are, in effect, *transgressing* the boundaries of the core theory in order to *correct* it, and thereby to save its normative appeal.

Rights and Freedom

At first glance, it may seem odd even to suggest a conflict between rights and freedom inasmuch as a major use of the concept of right is precisely to mark off an area in which an individual's freedom cannot rightfully be countermanded. Nonetheless, it must be realized that for a person to claim a right is, for most categories of rights, to claim a moral justification for limiting the freedom of

---

*For those categories of human beings that are excluded (in varying degrees) from possession of such rights—children, the mentally deficient, and so on—it must be concluded that their lives cannot be fulfilled precisely to the extent that they are incapable of forming and implementing individual "life plans." Paternalism in the liberal tradition is an expedient for helping those on the threshold or on the peripheries of full humanity. It is emphatically not a treatment deemed proper for human beings in general.

those to whom the rights claims are addressed. To have a right to limit others' freedom *de jure;* and, so far as rights are enforced by law, to limit their freedom *de facto* as well. Thus if I have a right to worship as I please (or not to worship at all), others (in this case, presumably, all others, whether or not they be agents of the state) are morally unfree to interfere with my actions in the matter of worship. Likewise, where there are thought to be rights to some benefits and burdens of citizenship, neither the state nor individuals acting outside the state apparatus can rightfully interfere with the enjoyment of such benefits or the exercise of such duties. And, finally, where it is claimed that there are rights to the enjoyment of some minimal level of social goods, to the extent such claims do specify correlative obligations, at least indirectly, they morally restrict the liberty of persons to act in violation of these obligations.

As we have seen, freedom for the liberal democrat is a social relation; one is free or unfree with respect to others. We have seen too how this view of freedom presupposes that our ends, ultimately, are incorrigible, how individuals are the final arbiters of their own ends. We know too that the incorrigibility of ends is not, by itself, sufficient for establishing an atomic individualist view of society, according to which the ultimate constituents of social reality (descriptively and normatively), the atoms, are individuals, essentially independent of one another and of society. The ends of atomic individuals are such that others figure only instrumentally in their realization. Where others figure essentially, as "ends-in-themselves" (Kant), atomic individualism does not pertain. It is clear then that atomic individualism does not follow from the incorrigibility of ends precisely because, if ends are incorrigible, no constraints are placed on their content. Thus rational agents might seek to realize ends that are altruistic or even social. They might value association or community. They might, therefore, even value others as "ends-in-themselves," and not as means only. But, as we have also seen, if this view of rational agency does not strictly entail atomic individualism, it inclines towards it. So far as there is no principle for bringing the individual's ends together into a common framework, analogous to Kant's "harmony of rational wills," so far as it is natural to regard everything and everyone as means for the satisfaction of antecedently given ends, things and persons *tend* to be treated the same way—as merely instrumental. The distinction one wants to draw between things and persons is effectively denied theoretical warrant.

And where individual behavior is construed as maximizing behavior aimed at doing as well *for oneself* as one can, at maximizing individuals' interests, the slide into atomic individualism is virtually insured. Then others effectively become means only; persons collapse into things. For such a theory, respect for persons, a sense of the pricelessness or intrinsic dignity of human beings, has no natural place.

Liberal democratic theory, with its core notions of freedom and interest, threatens to turn into a theory of just this sort. Unless its core is somehow supplemented with a corrective to what its core suggests about persons and their relations, liberal democratic theory will have little appeal for anyone, including virtually all liberal democrats, whose vision of proper political and social arrangements requires that these arrangements, however free and however conducive to maximizing social welfare, support, or at least not undermine, human dignity.

It is significant that throughout its history, critics of liberal democracy, from both the left and the right, have reproached liberal democratic theory for its atomic individualism, and for its corresponding inability to theorize persons as other than merely instrumental. No where is this kind of reproach more frequent and more telling than in critical reflections on "free markets." The conceptual possibility of non-market liberal democratic theories will be broached in Part III. Without intending to prejudice that discussion, it can now be noted that market arrangements do—as much as any institutional arrangements might—embody the core liberal democratic notions of freedom and interest. By definition, market exchanges are voluntary or freely chosen, and participants in market transactions, by hypothesis, seek to do as well for themselves as possible, given their interests, and given the constraint that others, with different and independent interests, also seek to do as well for themselves as they can.

In markets, products of labor exchange as commodities with determinant values measurable against other commodities. In capitalist markets—that is, in the form of market arrangements linked historically with the emergence and development of liberal democracy—labor too (or, as Marxists would prefer, "labor power") is a commodity. To the extent that the exchange of labor (or labor power) is subordinated to the requirements of capitalist accumulation, to the extent it is (in Marx's sense) exploitative, any difference in treatment between persons (as workers) and things (as products of labor) is effectively undone. Each becomes neither more nor less than a determinant exchange value, to be used as the accumulation process requires. It is this treatment of workers as means only that motivates well-known attacks on capitalist markets for producing "alienation,"[7] or for fragmenting and commercializing social life, thereby reducing the bases for social solidarity and even political legitimacy.[8] Despite very different political motivations, what such charges share is the realization that human dignity is jeopardized in capitalist markets: that the worker, in being treated as a commodity, becomes a thing, while the capitalist, the *homo oeconomicus*, subordinated to the requirements of capitalist calculation, reduces himself to an atomic individual for whom persons are means only and humanity—in himself as well as in others—disappears.

Historically committed to a view of human beings as acquisitive, rational egoists and therefore, at least tendentially, to atomic individualism, liberal democrats who rely on markets as institutional embodiments of liberal democratic ideals need the concept of (human) rights to save (free, self-interested) human beings from themselves, and thereby to maintain and promote human dignity. Without such rights, a free society of "rational economic agents" threatens to become a society of things, of instrumentalites; a collection of atomic individuals for whom every-

thing and everyone are means only. Rights claims—that is, claims
for inalienable (human) rights—counter this threat. Inalienable
rights *limit* markets.

By definition, inalienable rights cannot be bought or sold.
Neither are they, in general, subject to other market criteria: they
are distributed equally, rather than as incentives, and they are
exercised, at least theoretically, without monetary charge. The
possession of such rights, accordingly, limits not only the freedom
of others, but one's own freedom to *exchange* these rights, as one
could one's other possessions. Were we to deny that our freedom
is limited in this way, and assume that market relations pertain
even in the domain of "inalienable" rights, we should have to
conclude, in order to maintain a sense of the inalienability of these
rights, that they are literally priceless, that there is nothing in
principle for which they could reasonably—that is, advanta-
geously, given persons' interests—be exchanged. Roughly, such
a view would parallel the Kantian thesis that what is essentially
human has "dignity" (*Würde*), while all else has only an exchange
value or price (*Preis*). But for self-interested citizens of the sort
liberal democracies produce and liberal democratic theory countenances, this claim is plainly false. It is easy to show that an
exchange of many "inalienable" rights can increase the welfare
of both buyers and sellers.[9] This situation would pertain, in fact,
whenever an exchange of such rights for money (or for any other
commodity) is regarded by each of the parties as advantageous.
That there would then be a vast market in votes is easy to see; in
any large- or even middle-sized democracy, an individual's vote
counts for so little in the final determination of the social choice
that many (if not most) individuals would prefer virtually any
monetary compensation to the retention and exercise of the right
to vote. In all likelihood, though to a lesser degree, other "inalienable rights" too would eventually find their price. Thus where
inalienable rights are thought to pertain, it must be that markets
are excluded as illegitimate. In this way, the tendency to treat
persons as things is countervailed without recourse to psychology—indeed, in terms compatible with the characteristic view that

people are by nature acquisitive and "economic." It is, in brief, by stipulating inalienable (human) rights that liberal democratic theory meets the challenge posed to human dignity by human nature (or, more exactly, by what liberal democrats take human nature to be), a challenge aided and abetted by liberal democracy's distinctive notions of freedom and interest.

We have seen how the assertion of rights meets this challenge where market relations pertain. Markets, however, are just particularly clear institutional expressions of liberal democracy's core notions. More generally, the strategy of appealing to inalienable (human) rights is apt for countering the tendency of any properly liberal democratic institutions.

The Viability of Rights

Two important and overlapping uses for rights have so far been noted. Rights may be used to specify the traditional liberal freedoms and thus to restrict the scope of democratic collective choice. And rights may be used to save human dignity from the onslaught of atomic individualism, a view of human society powerfully suggested, though not strictly implied, by liberal democracy's core theory. This list is by no means exhaustive, but it is enough to indiciate the role rights can play in liberal democratic theory. If the concept is finally satisfactory, it can be used not only to solve the problems posed in chapter 5, but also to make liberal democratic theory an attractive and viable normative vision of a good society. The time has come, therefore, to determine if that concept is indeed satisfactory. Were Bentham and Mill right in deriding the concept of rights, and in insisting that there is no theoretically well-motivated way to assign "abstract right(s) as a thing independent of utility" to persons? If so, any uses liberal democrats or others make of the concept are arbitrary and therefore, finally, unsatisfactory. In what remains, I will suggest that Bentham and Mill very likely were right, and that if there is a non-arbitrary way to assign rights to persons, it has yet to be developed or even intimated.

As when they speak of "true" interests, liberal democrats could and sometimes do borrow eclectically from the idealist tradition, talking *as if* it were somehow possible to provide a specification of peoples' rights, independent of what people believe or want or, more generally, take their rights to be. Such borrowing from a different and incompatible tradition is, of course, irremediably *ad hoc*. But it is far from clear, even so, that this strategy will work for the purpose at hand. It is worth noting that idealist political theory, if it does not exclude talk of rights altogether, assigns a different and far less portentious role to rights than we find in the liberal democratic literature. The reason is plain: idealism makes use of a different notion of freedom. Where individual liberty is not conceived and valued as liberal democracy's core theory requires, moral justifications for restricting the liberty of others (in the Hobbesian-liberal sense) take on much diminished importance. And where human dignity is not threatened, as in liberalism, rights are not required as a counter-tendency. An eclectic amalgam of liberal democracy's core notions of freedom and interest and an idealist use of rights is an unlikely candidate for a coherent and adequate political theory. But a precondition, even for attempting such an unlikely project, is to develop what, for apparently good reason, has so far never been developed successfully: a theoretically well-motivated, idealist account of rights ascriptions of a sort that would restrict the scope of democratic collective choice and, at the same time, counter the tendency of liberal democratic theory and practice to obliterate the crucial difference between persons, as bearers of dignity, and mere things. It may be that for Locke and his contemporaries, the recourse to God as the source of rights is less a use of an antiquated metaphysics than a desperate expedient. Contemporary neo-Lockeans seem not even to have this fragile support.[10]

Ultimately, then, in just the way that liberalism's efforts to ascribe interests to persons fails on grounds of arbitrariness or lack of theoretical warrant, so too does the recourse to rights. To be sure, if we are content to appeal, as many do, to a (presumed) consensus on rights ascriptions, it may be that rights do fulfill their intended functions tolerably well. But they do not do so from the critical vantage point liberalism as a substantive and radical social theory, requires. If rights claims rest on consensus, they cannot be used to evaluate that consensus. They cannot function critically.

We saw in the last chapter that Mill's use of the private/public distinction to restrict the respective scopes of the liberal and democratic components was either arbitrary (lacking theoretical justification) or circular (depending on norms and intuitions that are themselves to be evaluated). We now see that the analogous strategy of appealing to rights runs afoul of the same dilemma. Unless rights can somehow be ascribed to persons independently and justifiably, the liberal democrat's use of rights fares no better, in the end, than Mill's bolder efforts to mark off the private sphere.

I have not shown that rights claims cannot be properly specified, but only that they have not yet been and that there is no inkling as to how they might be. Borrowing from idealism will not work, and neither, I would hazard, will appealing to heaven. Drawing on our intuitions may work for many practical purposes, but not for addressing the problems posed in chapter 5. And for defending human dignity, this is a shallow foundation indeed.

The liberal democrat's use of rights, even if ultimately unsuccessful, is nonetheless instructive. As we have seen, it is human rights that provide liberal democracy with a "human face." The recourse to rights is interesting, then, primarily for what it reveals about the political tradition in which rights claims operate. The liberal democratic use of rights is *symptomatic* of a tension between human dignity and liberal democracy's core theory. Human rights claims function within liberalism as a corrective, an element introduced apart from the core theory, with a view to countervailing some of its less savory consequences. But ultimately this corrected liberalism is a *contradictory* configuration, simultaneously defending and attacking human dignity, distinguishing and confounding persons and things.

Human rights save us from our institutions and their *effects* upon ourselves. Were our institutions otherwise, were they of a sort to promote social solidarity and treatment of persons as ends, then the need for human rights would diminish accordingly. Doubtless, this is one reason why human rights play no role in (idealist) political visions such as Rousseau's in *The Social Contract*, where the institutions of society work together to form "the general will," by promoting virtue and citizenship and thus undoing that individualism that, on Rousseau's account, threatens what is essentially human. For Rousseau, the alternative to rights claims is education: education in the broadest sense, by no means limited to the schools, that transforms a collection of atomic individuals (such as emerge from the state of nature) into a body politic wherein, so to speak, human dignity is inscribed in each person's will. In this *de jure* state, human rights drop away for want of sufficient reason as much as for want of theoretical justification.

However, within the framework of liberal democratic institutions, so far from "withering away," the need for human rights is intensified. Doubtless this need will persist so long as political arrangements, unlike those Rousseau envisioned, coordinate independent and (sometimes) conflicting rather than harmonious interests, "private" rather than "general" wills. But there is no reason to suppose that this function can only be fulfilled by the concept of human rights, that in the framework of a theory and practice of politics outside the dominant, liberal democratic tradition, what human rights claims articulate might not be theorized differently and without arbitrariness. It must be acknowledged, of course, that the theoretical apparatus for fulfilling this function outside the dominant tradition remains largely undeveloped, particularly if we are skeptical of the sort of "education" Rousseau and other idealists propose. But the theoretical vulnerability of human rights claims—and of the dominant tradition generally—renders the need for investigating alternatives crucial. It is in this sense, and to this end, that the criticism of human rights need not be incompatible with their defense. Ultimately, I think, the best defense of human rights or, rather, of what they aim to articulate is their *reconceptualization* and implementation in the framework of a different—and yet to be developed—politics, with institutions embodying a different tendency, a tendency to promote social solidarity and respect for persons and thus to realize in different ways what, against the tendency of liberal democracy's core theory, human rights claims assert.

Again, it is not my intention to endorse idealist political thought, but I would suggest that for this issue particularly, for the reconceptualization of human rights, there is a good deal more to learn from idealism than from the well-intentioned, but troubled, dominant tradition.

Prospects for the Liberal Democratic Project

Whatever may ultimately be the fate of the concept of rights and of the dominant tradition, it is clear that *within* the tradition, so long as rights cannot be ascribed from the elusive critical vantage point substantive liberalism requires, rights will work no better than interests for rendering the liberal demoratic project coherent. In whatever other ways the concept may prove useful (or useless) for liberal democracy, it apparently will not serve to establish the respective scopes of liberal democracy's components.

Under what conditions, then, does the unlikely project of combining liberalism and democracy appear feasible and even attractive? In view of what has been shown to this point, it would seem unlikely that it could ever be either. Yet liberal democracy, as we know, has established virtual hegemony over political life for more than a century. It has appeared feasible and attractive, and it continues, whatever theoretical and practical "crises" liberalism or democracy suffer, to provide many thinkers and virtually all politicians (in the mainstream of Western political life) with their vision, such as it it is, of proper and good political arrangements.

I would suggest that this dominance over political life is a consequence of historical circumstances that effectively mitigate the full implementation of a central element of the liberal democratic core theory, its notion of popular sovereignty. Popular sovereignty is of course never abandoned explicitly. Were it so, liberal democracy's affinities to the democratic tradition would be severed, and the rationale for liberal democratic theory would be, to that extent, undone. But the abandonment of popular sovereignty is nonetheless real.

That popular sovereignty is indeed abandoned, in practice but not in theory, is evident, I think, if we focus, at last, on those characteristic institutions of liberal democratic polities—representative government and its attendant institutional support, the party system. To this point, it seems that liberal democrats ought to favor direct democratic control, not representative government, over whatever falls within the proper domain of democratic collective choice, and that the nearly universal recourse to representative institutions represents, at most, a concession to the impracticability of direct democracy. Representative government, in short, seems to be a satisfactory compromise between the core theory and practicality. We shall now examine that "compromise." It is, I will argue, of far greater moment than first appears.

8 / Representation

LIBERAL democracy's core theory rests on popular sovereignty and direct democratic rule. The rationale for the democratic component virtually requires direct democracy, for it is thought that individual interests are best served—with a view to achieving the aggregative maximum—when each individual, considered the best judge of his own interests, figures equally in the determination of the social choice. Yet virtually without exception, liberal democrats never advocate direct democracy. On the contrary, their commitment has always been to representative government. The institutional implementation of this commitment varies considerably from polity to polity, but the general contours of liberal democratic representative government remain the same nearly everywhere. The people do not legislate directly, but through legislators, who generally are vested with considerable and sometimes even complete independence to legislate for those whom they represent. Citizens vote on legislators, not on matters for legislation. Thus they control legislation only indirectly, or, as is sometimes said, through "consent," registered in periodic (and generally infrequent) elections in which, by either returning or refusing to return their elected representatives to office, they rule on what these legislators have done on their behalf. It is plain that legislators are only very tenuously controlled by those whom they represent. Of far greater importance in directing the legislative process, and even in selecting candidates for legislatures, are political parties and related institutions that effectively mediate between the sovereign people and their government.

It is clear that there is, at best, a tension between the theoretical commitments of the core theory and their proposed embodiments in representative governments. It is remarkable, indeed, that this tension is not more widely noted and reflected upon. But, as we have seen, liberal democrats characteristically avoid the most fundamental questions of political philosophy, and nowhere more so than in regard to the democratic component. Thus liberal democrats, almost without exception, overlook the problem their advocacy of representative government poses. However, it is precisely the connection between liberal democracy and democracy as such that representative government, though widely and even enthusiastically endorsed by liberal democrats, puts into question. We shall see that the apparently innocuous issue of political representation is in fact the key for uncovering, at once, the essentially undemocratic character of liberal democracy and also the "solution" to the conceptual problems posed in chapter 5.

Some Simple but False Justifications for Representative Government

How can democrats justify representative government or, indeed, anything less than direct democratic control? Rousseau thought they could not. Liberal democrats, however, are as a rule quite confident that representative institutions do accord well with their theoretical commitments as democrats. Thus if they confront the problem at all, they finds its solution easy.

There are a number of ready justifications for representative government, of which the most immediate is that, in virtually all existing polities, direct democratic rule is impracticable, while representative government, on the contrary, is eminently practicable and serves the same purpose, at least tolerably well. Viable political units, it is maintained, are in general too large for direct democracy to work. It would be difficult, if not impossible, even to assemble the citizenry of an actual state, and absolutely impossible to sustain rational deliberation among such multitudes, as the process of legislation requires. Representative government, however, is held to be a workable approximation of the impractical, direct democratic ideal. Its justification, then, is that it ensures the realization of democratic values that could not practically be realized otherwise. Were it workable, direct democracy would be preferable. But direct democracy is not workable. Therefore representative government, and its attendant institutional complements, emerges as our best feasible alternative.

To be sure, this kind of argument suggests a picture of the representative quite different from what which liberal democrats characteristically endorse. If representative institutions are just workable approximations of direct democratic voting, representatives, it would seem, should act as delegates only, slavishly transmitting the choices of the citizens they represent. But liberal democrats almost never regard representatives as simple conduits for communicating the choices of their constituents. They view representatives, instead, as independent legislators, voting according to their own best judgment. This view of the independence of representatives may well be at odds with the justification for representative government just sketched, but it is an entirely understandable move. The independence of representatives is itself a consequence of the impracticability of direct democracy. Representatives cannot always ascertain the will of their constituents in a regular and systematic way, and therefore must act with a measure of independence. Perhaps liberal democrats ought to deplore this fact, and seek to minimize its impact. Many, however, go on to make a virtue of necessity. But even for these enthusiasts, the independence of representatives, like representative government itself, is hardly a positive good, but a concession to the unwieldy realities of modern political life.

This argument is plausible and would, I think, be widely acknowledged. But it does not adequately reconstruct the principal liberal democratic view. For liberal democracy does not, characteristically, view representative institutions as necessary evils or second-best approximations to an unworkable ideal. On the contrary, representative government is widely depicted as the ideal form of political organization, and, strikingly, even as the proper institutional embodiment of popular sovereignty! For most liberal democrats, representative government is not at all a concession to the difficulties of practical political life, but is itself the ideal. Thus the justification for representative government that appeals to the unworkability of direct democracy is, at best, incomplete. More likely, as I will go on to argue, it is a superficial and even *ad hoc* consideration that helps liberal democrats overcome a profound, and largely unacknowledged, divergence between the theory of liberal democracy and its practice.

Another ready answer is that representative institutions support the implementation of liberal values better than do alternative direct democratic ones. Many liberal democrats advance this view in one version or another. But it is hardly a properly liberal democratic position. For the rationale that underlies this justification for representative institutions depends on an anti-democratic distrust of the people and their collective choices; it is therefore out of phase, at best, with the spirit and intent of liberal democracy's theory. The great fear is that the assembled people will prove mercurial and capricious, that they will lack the civility and good sense necessary for legislating wisely, and will thus become easy targets for demagogues and tyrants. Volatile popular assemblies, it is feared, will transgress the boundaries of democratic collective choice (assuming, as seems unlikely, such boundaries can be constructed), and will trample upon the "rights" liberal democrats want to protect. Representative governments, on the other hand, will be much less likely to do so, it is supposed, for they are thought to embody the political virtues of civility and good sense, and to be steady and cautious in abiding by the constitutional arrangements of liberal democratic polities. However, liberal democrats, if they are to be democrats, must trust the people and distrust professional legislators who rule on their behalf. This trust is a consequence of the rationale that supports the democratic component. Ruling well, to be sure, means protecting individuals' freedoms (rights), but it also means optimizing interest satisfaction, within the parameters of collective, political life. Ruling well does not mean ruling according to some ideal standard of proper statecraft, against which the actual performance of governments may be assessed. For liberal democrats, again, there are no ideal standards. There are only individuals' interests, reducible ultimately to their wants. And, in the final analysis, the individual, not his representative, is the best judge of his own interests. Despite what many liberal democratic writers may think and even say, there is no way, consonant with the core theory, to regard representative government more highly than direct democracy for promoting individuals' interests. Indeed, the contrary is the case. Liberal democrats, then, should be disposed to trust the people. And they should be disposed to distrust any government that, in effect, substitutes its will for that of the sovereign people. Like all liberals, liberal democrats should of course be ever vigilant in the protection and defense of liberty. Liberals should fear the encroachments of all governments, including those that arrive at collective choices directly and democratically. "The tyranny of the majority" is indeed a threat to liberty. But representative government is hardly a counter to this threat. For there is no reason to trust representatives, or anyone else, better than the people themselves, even for the protection of liberties. As democrats, liberal democrats should trust the people, and *a fortiori* trust them to protect liberty.*

If we attend, then, to the logic of the liberal democratic position, rather than to the express or implicit pronouncements of liberal democrats, it is clear that neither the unworkability of direct democracy in existing, large-scale political entities, nor the liberal democrat's commitment to liberal values, will suffice to explain the nearly universal appeal of representative institutions

---

*See chapter 5. In the final analysis, the victory of liberal values will be assured only through the transformation of the citizenry into liberals, by education (in the broadest sense) in liberal values. For liberal democrats, respect for privacy (in Mill's sense) cannot be legislated; it can only be inculcated, if at all, as an effect of the proper workings of liberal institutions, transforming generations of men and women into citizens who, above all, regard their own and each other's privacy as inviolable.

for liberal democrats. To uncover the role representation plays in liberal democratic theory, we must, as it were, look beneath these immediate, but superficial and misleading justifications.

Why Representation?

A more pertinent explanation for the appeal of representative institutions is the underlying inclination of liberal democrats to distinguish the social from the political, to the detriment of the latter (see chapter 1). Civil society, not the state, is the sphere of human self-fulfillment, the arena where human energies are best and most productively expended. To devote time and attention to legislation, then, is to drain energy away from where it is best employed. It is to squander on the state, a necessary evil, energy that could be expended usefully in society, in the pursuit of individual satisfactions. It is therefore best to minimize citizens' participation in the governmental process. To do so is to contain political life, as it should be contained, to the barest minimum. So far as possible, consonant with the other theoretical commitments liberal democrats hold, individuals should be left free to pursue their private ends. Where citizens govern directly, the state is expanded—unnecessarily—at society's expense. But neither can citizens entirely relinquish control over their own governance. Thus representative government emerges as the best solution to a twin exigency. Citizens are governed, but by their representatives, that is, by persons of their own choosing. Thus, it seems, participation is minimized, while democratic control is retained.

In consequence political participation ceases to be a duty of citizenship, except very tenuously and indirectly, as when citizens are encouraged or even required to vote for their representatives. Instead, politics becomes a special vocation, a career among many. And even for the professional politician, political participation has no special role, as is thought throughout many other traditions of political theory, in fulfilling man's fate as a *zoón politikon*, a political animal. The professional politician is, above all, a careerist, working perhaps with a view to doing good as a public administrator or legislator, but, as in any career, working primarily with a view to doing well for himself. In this way, society triumphs not only over the state, but even over the institutions of government. In professionalizing politics, representative government minimizes political participation at the same time as it transforms its character—from the principal expression of each individual's essential humanity to a vocation among many.

Thus the tension already examined between liberal democracy's liberal and democratic components here reappears as a tension between that tendency, fundamental to liberalism, to expand the social at the expense of the political, and liberal democracy's theoretical commitments to popular sovereignty and democratic collective choice. This shift, I think, points to the hidden agenda that motivates the liberal democrat's enthusiastic allegiance to representative institutions in the face of a justifying theory that, at best, inclines against it.

It is this hidden agenda that makes political representation so important for liberal democratic theory, and so interesting philosophically. Whatever practicing liberal democrats may think or say to account for the appeal of representative institutions, the role these institutions play in liberal democratic polities is very largely to alleviate the tension between liberalism and democracy by *displacing* it, as it were, from theory to practice, from a matter of an elusive conceptual coherence to a practical question of the character and functioning of the institutions of government. If liberalism and democracy as such cannot properly coexist, then one or the other must somehow give. It is, significantly, the democratic component that proves vulnerable and gives way in practice. Liberal democrats are, after all, liberals first, and democrats only reluctantly. Popular sovereignty and direct control figure in liberal democratic *theory* as requirements, as it were, of the conceptual framework in which liberal democrats conceive politics. But *in practice* they are expressly abandoned (direct democratic rule) or effectively undone (popular sovereignty).

Thus the theoretical problem of joining liberalism and democracy remains unsolved. But that problem pales into unimportance when liberal democracy's theoretical commitments are implemented in representative institutions. What is theoretically insoluble is somehow satisfactorily addressed in practice; the integrity of liberal democracy, as a body of discourse and as a political practice, seems vindicated after all. However this "solution" is illusory. It is in fact no solution at all. Representative institutions, far from implementing, even approximately, the democratic values liberal democrats are committed to, in fact betray these values.

What is betrayed is the liberal democratic justification for the democratic component: that democratic collective choice is justified for maximizing interest satisfaction, and thus for yielding optimal levels of social welfare. This justification is of course not expressly repudiated. On the contrary, liberal democrats doubtless think representative institutions contribute to the attainment of the aggregative ideals they profess. The repudiation is practical and unacknowledged, and in no way part of liberal democracy's justifying theory. That this repudiation is nonetheless real may be appreciated by considering some important differences between representative and direct democratic government. Some of these differences are, so to speak, natural but not strictly logical consequences of the functioning of representative institutions. In theory, then, these differences are eliminable, though, by all evidence, their elimination is exceedingly unlikely. Other differences follow logically, and therefore unavoidably, from the nature of representative government.

We know that liberalism and democracy can be combined only if the scope of democratic collective choice is restricted to provide for the proper sphere of individual prerogative that defines the liberal component. And we have seen that a theoretically well-motivated way to restrict the scope of democratic collective choice remains an elusive ideal of liberal democratic theory. However, as the historical experience of representative government in liberal democratic polities attests, representative institutions *in them-selves* restrict the scope of democratic choice. That they do so is a universal fact, the explanation for which doubtless consists, in part, in the virtual impossibility of a relatively few professional politicians ruling over all matters that fall in the public sphere and that are plausibly candidates for collective choice. In other words, representative institutions vastly over-restrict the scope of democratic choice. The core theory, in effect, requires many more votes than the institutions of representative government can reasonably support. Thus, contrary to what democrats—and, therefore, liberal democrats—would want, the characteristic institutional apparatus of liberal democratic polities effectively removes large areas of public life from public debate and collective control, indeed, even from the kind of indirect control the citizenry retains under representative government. The citizenry effectively relinquishes control over many matters that affect it publicly and that it therefore *ought* to control, precisely because these matters cease to be objects of public choice at all.

We know too that in existing liberal democratic polities, virtually without exception, the executive branch of government has come to grow at the expense of the legislative, both in parliamentary systems of government and in states, like the United States, that constitutionally uphold a separation of powers. Since in general even indirect control over the executive functions of government is far weaker than over the legislative, popular control over matters of public pertinence is further diminished. That this process occurs universally is a good indication of its unavoidability, even if it is not, strictly, implied by the existence of representative government.

It is because representative institutions effectively remove so much from collective choice that they are particularly appropriate in societies where market transactions dominate social life. Many outcomes of market transaction—particularly where markets govern the production and distribution of goods—fall unequivocally in the public sphere. Inasmuch as individuals' interests are vitally concerned, decisions about production and distribution ought, presumably, to be made democratically. However market trans-actions are, by definition, consentual and bilateral. They are not publicly debated, except perhaps incidentally, and they are never determined by votes. Where markets organize behavior, political control is absent. Representative government encourages this ab-sence.

By itself, the advocacy of market relations is not at all un-democratic. Quite the contrary. Market transactions are paradig-matically democratic, at least in the minimal sense reconstructed by Arrow social welfare functions. Free markets satisfy the Pareto condition and the condition on Non-Dictatorship—the two con-ditions that (minimally) reconstruct what it is to decide demo-cratically—as well as the other conditions Arrow stipulates for formulating the problem of collective choice. Moreover, markets are plausibly thought to promote social welfare. As is well known, there is a long tradition of argument, dating back at least to Adam Smith, that maintains that market transactions, if left free to run their course, lead directly to the optimal level of social welfare. The operative intuition, it seems, is that where persons act vol-untarily and as utility maximizers, they will enter into bilateral agreements only if these agreements leave them better off, given their interests, than they would otherwise be. For this reason, wherever market relations pertain, in helping oneself one inad-vertently helps others. And social welfare—the sum of individ-uals' welfares—is maximized, accordingly, as individuals maxi-mize their own welfares.

A problem with the invisible hand argument is that it pre-supposes an initial distribution of assets which does not itself result from bilateral voluntary transfers, and which has welfare effects. If the initial distribution is not optimal, then there is no reason to think optimality will be achieved by subsequent trans-actions. A further problem is that the invisible hand argument ignores the effects, measurable as costs or benefits, of bilateral decisions on third parties who are not part of these agreements, and who cannot plausibly be said to have consented to them. It can be shown that under highly restrictive and unrealistic assumptions, "external effects," as these effects on third parties are called, can be handled by market mechanisms; costs and benefits can be accounted for properly through bilateral agreements. In the real world of liberal democratic politics, however, external effects generally cannot be handled at all satisfactorily without substantial state intervention; it is far from clear, even so, that they can be handled at all. Thus the supposed aggregative advantages of market arrangements in real world contexts are dubious, at best— even if, strictly speaking, free markets do aggregate individuals' choices democratically.

It may be that the case for markets is overwhelming, nonetheless (see chapter 9). However this may be, for many, if not most, matters of vital importance to wide portions of the citizenry, democratic voting, not bilateral negotiations leading to market transactions, seems clearly the best course. Wherever democratic collective choices are to be made, voting is a reasonable—and often the most reasonable—way to make these choices. To be sure, the very notion of democratic collective choice is problematic (see chapter 3). But if we bracket our hesitations on this score, voting seems the most attractive way to achieve the optimal level of social welfare, where the interests of large numbers of people are affected, directly or indirectly, by the social choice.

As liberals, liberal democrats have a plausible case for advocating the extension of market relations. Markets limit the sphere of direct political coercion and therefore, it might be argued, extend the range of individual liberty, in strict accordance with liberalism's presumptive case for extending liberty as far as possible and therefore for restricting the power of the state to what is minimally necessary for insuring that degree of order without which the optimal level of freedom cannot be realized. On the other hand, as democrats, liberal democrats have a case for extending the scope of voting, and thus of political determination, to the limit of the proper boundaries of democratic choice. These positions are plainly opposed. And this opposition is plainly a manifestation of the opposition already noted between liberalism and democracy, now displaced onto the question of the extent of political control or, what comes to the same thing, the degree of society's dominance of the state. Given the liberal democrat's deeply entrenched view of the relation between politics and society, it is hardly surprising that liberal democrats should resolve this tension on the side of liberalism or society, rather than democracy or the state. As we have seen, representative government and its attendant institutions are, in essence, the institutional embodiment of this resolution, a resolution entirely at democracy's expense.

Democracy cannot but suffer by the very nature of representative institutions. Whether or not, as is everywhere the case, representative government contracts the role of the state beyond what the democratic tradition encourages, the shift from direct to representative legislatures, and therefore the transformation of the citizen from direct legislator to conferrer of consent upon the choices of others, fundamentally violates the case for the democratic component. Whatever liberal democrats may say or believe, conferring consent by participating in elections for representatives—particularly when elections are infrequent and periodic, as is nearly everywhere the rule—is in no way even a remote approximation of choosing for oneself among alternative options for collective choice. Arguably, citizens of representative "democracies" select their rulers. But they do not themselves rule, as any properly liberal democratic theory requires. We have seen that Rousseau long ago pointed out that representative government is not at all an approximation of direct democracy, but something quite different and even incompatible. We can now see that Rousseau was right; representative governments cannot allow for the aggregation of citizens' choices in the way adherents of popular sovereignty and therefore of popular control require.[2]

Where the point is to achieve the aggregative maximum, each individual ought to make his own choices because, in general, each individual is the best judge of his own interests. To entrust legislation to representatives is to relinquish to others our concern for furthering our own interests. In doing so, inevitably, we diminish individual and therefore also social welfare. Still, there may be good reasons, perhaps even good liberal democratic reasons, for turning to representative government. We have in passing already noted several: to faciliate orderly and efficient government, to protect against the real or imagined tyranny of volatile and capricious majorities, perhaps even to facilitate and encourage the dominance of society over the state. But however attractive these reasons or others that might be advanced on behalf of political representation might be for liberal democrats, they ultimately contradict what motivates the liberal democrat's allegiance to the democratic tradition. Liberal democrats can overlook this contradiction, if their determination to do so is sufficiently powerful, as it seems to have been throughout liberal democracy's long career. But this contradiction has political consequences. Thus liberal democracies are, as it were despite their justifying theory, if not quite anti-democratic, hardly good examples of ongoing democratic politics.

Liberal democratic political arrangements have been faulted, by Marxists and others, for maintaining the form, but not the substance of popular sovereignty and democratic control. The distinction between form and substance in which this criticism is couched may be obscure and even misleading, but the intent of the complaint is clear enough. In liberal democratic polities there are periodic elections in which everyone (or nearly everyone) may vote—but even so, what the state does is barely, if at all, a function of individuals' choices.* This line of criticism converges with the position developed here. Liberal democracy exists, I have maintained, at the expense of its democratic component. While presenting itself as, at once, both liberal and democratic, liberal democracy is in fact liberal really and democratic only apparently. Appearance to the contrary, it falls outside the democratic camp. Liberal democracy's putative and apparent links with the demo-

*It is then sometimes argued that a government of elected representatives can and in fact often does serve as a mechanism through which a ruling class (which is by no means identical with the elected representatives of the enfranchised people) organizes its domination over other classes. Some facets of this claim will be addressed, and substantially endorsed, in chapter 10.

cratic tradition are by no means idle, as I shall go on to suggest. But these links are nonetheless illusory. If by faulting liberal democracy for the merely formal character of its democratic institutions, critics mean that there is only the appearance, but not the substance of democratic control, their criticism, I think, is entirely apt.

We know that many liberal democrats see no conflict and perhaps even no tension between democracy and representative government. Representative institutions are sometimes even claimed to implement traditional notions of popular sovereignty, and thus to be the proper contemporary form of democratic rule. Inasmuch as these connections are in fact illusory, if we are to understand their character and role, we must look to their political functioning, not their express theoretical content. Evidently, the claim that representative institutions are democratic serves to mystify the character of these institutions, and in so doing to legitimize them. In depicting representative government—falsely and misleadingly—as a workable approximation of direct democratic control, democratic legitimacy, so to speak, is conferred on these institutions. The people seem to rule; hence the institutional arrangements of liberal democratic states seem to serve liberal democrats' aggregative ideals. In this way, support for representative institutions is maintained. The mantle of popular sovereignty is taken on by what, in fact, undoes liberal democracy's practical affinity to the democratic tradition.

Thus while subscribing to a theory of popular sovereignty, liberal democracy, at the same time, undercuts its functioning. The affinity between prevailing, liberal democratic institutions and their justifying theory is therefore fundamentally equivocal. And it is this equivocation, in the end, that is the condition for the possibility of the liberal democratic project. Appearance and also the express declarations of liberal democrats to the contrary, the liberal democratic project is feasible only at the tremendous cost, indeed the impossible cost for any democrat, of abandoning the substance of the democratic component.

Part III / Liberal Democracy as Politics

IT was suggested in Part I that liberal democratic theory is vulnerable in light of some of its most fundamental presuppositions. Then in Part II, I argued that the project of combining liberalism and democracy is theoretically unworkable and, therefore, politically practicable only at the expense of one or the other—in fact, always the democratic—component. In this final section, I will propose a rather different kind of complaint. Most generally, my claim is that, whatever its theoretical merits or shortcomings, the real world impact of liberal democratic theory is radically defective. I will develop two related versions of this charge: that liberal democratic theory is inadequate—both as a theory of existing arrangements and as a normative ideal—in virtue of its *abstractness*, its failure to focus on the institutional context within which liberal and democratic ideals operate, and that liberal democratic theory is at fault for its conceptual, and not merely historical, links with capitalism. Consideration of these criticisms will provide a context for speculating on the possibilities for "revisionist liberalisms," that seek to remedy liberal democracy's real world failings while retaining conceptual continuity with its core theory.

As a genre of criticism, the sort in question here is, I think, the most straight-forwardly political and also the most unambiguously left-wing. Those who would fault liberal democracy's model of society or its account of human nature might as well draw conservative as "progressive" conclusions from these complaints. They might criticize the dominant tradition in order to espouse ideals proper to genuine conservative political theory: values such as community (in place of association through market relations), and ideals of human behavior such as loyalty and a sense of status or place (as opposed to the unremitting maximizing behavior liberal democrats think natural and rational). Likewise, those who would grant liberal democracy's internal incoherence and its effective, though unacknowledged, undermining of popular sovereignty might as well applaud as deplore this fatal moderation of the liberal democrat's commitment to democratic collective choice. But to fault liberal democratic theory for abstracting from institutional arrangements, and for its links to capitalism, is to attack liberal democracy plainly from the left. Whatever else it may do, liberal democratic theory today functions conservatively, to support existing social practices and to block radical change.*

Many more issues will be raised here than can be adequately investigated. The character of the conceptual connections between liberal democracy nd capitalism is exceedingly complex. What follows is intended, in part, as a contribution towards clarifying some of the issues involved, but it will by no means exhaust all facets of the question, nor even bear upon many of its important aspects. What is directly under discussion here is not so much liberal democracy and capitalism *per se*, as the adequacy of the liberal democratic account of political arragements, in the light of some demonstrable connections between liberal democracy and capitalism.

Chapter 9 illustrates what is intended by the charge of ab-

---

*Two points already made in passing should be recalled here: the complaint, registered in chapter 2, that liberalism's distinctive concept of freedom, as traditionally understood, denies the role of existing institutional arrangements in restricting liberty, and the claim, discussed in chapter 8, that the liberal democrat's commitment to representative institutions effectively weights the social choice mechanism of liberal democratic politics decisively in the direction of maintaining existing arrangements. Both points are, in effect, instances of the kind of criticism to be developed below. And each, from a political point of view, faults liberal democratic theory's implicit commitment to maintaining the status quo.

stractness, focusing on voluntary transactions of the kind liberals (and, therefore, liberal democrats) deem particularly legitimate precisely because they are, by the liberal account, paradigmatically free—though many might find them objectionably exploitative. I will argue that liberal democratic theory cannot adequately account for voluntary, exploitative exchange, in virtue of its abstractness, and that this is indeed a defect of the theory. I will also resume briefly the discussion of freedom begun in chapter 2; for in reflecting on voluntary, exploitative exchange, we will have occasion to wonder why liberals are, as a rule, so reluctant to think of levels or degrees of freedom. Then in chapter 10, I will examine the one sustained effort so far undertaken to remedy these and other defects without breaking radically from the conceptual framework of liberal democratic theory: C. B. Macpherson's "nonmarket theory of democracy." Examination of Macpherson's contribution is apt, not just for the intrinsic importance of his work, but for the light it sheds both on the conceptual possibility and also, more importantly, the politics that motivates efforts to go *beyond* liberal democracy, without breaking radically from its theory and practice.

9 / Freedom and Exploitation

MANY writers have noted a close, historical association between liberal democracy and capitalism.[1] Sometimes it is said that capitalism could not have emerged without liberal democratic political institutions or, more strictly, their anticipations in early modern European polities. However, in light of the many contemporary schemes for capitalist "development" in countries whose institutions are not even remotely liberal or democratic, the case for this claim, as a general rule about liberal democracy and capitalism, is very doubtful to say the least. More often, the converse is claimed: that liberal democracy required capitalism for its emergence and that liberal democratic institutions could not long survive capitalism's demise. These hypothesized connections between liberal democracy and capitalism have been adduced, depending on the views of those who advance one or another of these claims, for or against capitalism; or, much more rarely, for or against liberal democracy.

That liberal democracy and capitalism are linked historically is, I think, beyond dispute, at least for the European and North American cases; it is, after all, only in these parts of the world that liberal democracy and capitalism developed, as it were, endogenously. However what is to be made of this historical connection is anything but clear. As already noted, the question is multi-faceted and complex, and it is not at all my intention to address it exhaustively. I will focus just on an issue that comes up often in considerations of the connection between freedom (in the liberal democratic sense) and capitalism: the concept of exploitation, particulary in the context of exchange relations. My reason for focusing just on this aspect of the broader question is, as will become evident, the light it sheds on the conceptual character of the liberal component. That discussion and those objectives, in turn, prompt a brief return to the subject of chapter 2, the Hobbesian and liberal concept of freedom, and to a theme of chapter 8, the gap between liberal democratic theory and practice.

It will be convenient to begin by looking at the liberal case, not for capitalism as such, but for markets.

Markets

Markets are systems of exchange in which goods and services (or money) are transferred through voluntary, bilateral agreements. Thus distribution is arranged exclusively by the parties concerned; neither custom nor law determines who gets what (though, of course, custom and law may regulate market behavior). Ultimately, the parties to market transactions themselves determine the societal distribution—in accordance with their interests.

To restrict voluntary transactions, whether by law or custom, would appear to be an unwarranted (and, therefore, objectionable) restriction on the liberty of those who would undertake the proposed transaction.[2] I want to suggest that this view is misleading because the real world context within which market transactions occur is systematically overlooked. To support this view, I will focus on the concept of exploitation—in the context of exchange relations.* To say of an exchange that it is exploitative is to impugn it as unjust. I will maintain that, to its fault, such charges of injustice cannot properly be accommoodated within the conceptual framework of liberal democratic theory. And I will suggest that this failing is a consequence of a general and pervasive characteristic of liberalism and, therefore, of liberal democratic theory:

---

*As will be evident further on, my intent is not in fact to endorse the concept of voluntary, exploitative exchange, but only to defend its coherence (and possible applicability) in the face of (largely implicit) liberal arguments to the contrary. It may be, as I shall go on to discuss, that the concept is vulnerable on other grounds.

its *abstractness* and thoroughgoing neglect of the world in which it functions as an effective presence and as a justifying theory. Abstractness is not, strictly, a requirement of the core theory. But I will argue that, even so, it is non-eliminable, so long as the liberal democratic project is maintained.

An exchange will count as *voluntary* only if all parties to it are free not to participate. And a person will be free not to participate whenever his participation is unconstrained by the effective interference of others. Thus, as discussed in chapter 2, freedom is a social relation: one is free (to do what one wants) with respect to other persons, and unfree when prevented by others from doing what one wants. A voluntary exchange, then, is an exchange where, with respect to the transaction in question, no party is unfree.*

To call an exchange exploitative is also to refer to the social relations pertaining among the participating parties. An exploitative exchange is, first of all, always an unequal exchange: an exchange in which the exploited party receives less than he gives to the exploiter. This is why charges of exploitation are tantamount to charges of injustice (unfairness). However not all unequal (unfair) exchanges are exploitative. To count as exploitative, a further condition must be satisfied: the exchange must *result from* social relations of unequal power. The exploiter and the exploited do not confront one another as equals. Among equals, net transfers can occur to the benefit of one or the other party for many reasons: trickery, good fortune, skill in bargaining and so on. These reasons

---

*As Aristotle remarks in the *Nicomachean Ethics* (book III, ch.1), a great deal that we would normally construe as involuntary action is, in fact, voluntary relative to specified constraints. It might be thought, for example, that no one, to use Aristotle's example, would voluntarily dispose of all his property, "for in the abstract no one throws goods away voluntarily." But "on condition of its securing the safety of himself (as in a storm) . . . any sensible man does so." What is relevant, then, in ascertaining when exchanges are voluntary is specifying the pertinent constraints. For liberals, these constraints are just those that would count for rendering persons unfree. Again, an action is voluntary if and only if, in the sense specified in chapter 2, the parties involved in the exchange are not, with respect to the exchange in question, unfree.

may be operative also in exchanges among unequal parties. But an exchange is exploitative only if the unequal power relation itself accounts for the net transfer. (Of course the unequal power relation that motivates the exchange need not be global, pertaining to the role of the exploited and exploiter in the entire social structure, but only unequal with respect to the proposed transaction.)

Liberals do, of course, recognize instances of exploitation, and even of exploitative exchange. But they endeavor to construe these instances as deviations from the market norm. Thus exploitative exchanges are typically conjured away, so to speak, by assimilation to models of unequal exchange that are plainly non-voluntary.

Not all models of unequal exchange can be used for this end. Bribery can be ruled out immediately, inasmuch as it need not result from unequal power relations. Fraud involves differential control of information (pertaining to the exchange in question), but such control typically does not, and certainly need not, result from *social* relations of unequal power. Moreover, in the kinds of exchange usually deemed exploitative, the victim is not tricked into entering into the transaction, as in cases of fraud; but does so knowingly and even wisely (given his interests), because the proposed exchange is the best available option.

A more likely model for construing away alleged cases of exploitation is taxation. Taxation plainly does involve social relations of unequal power (between the government and its citizens), and it is surely an unequal exchange. However exploitation cannot be reduced to taxation, since only the state (or some other *de facto* authority) can levy taxes, while the kinds of exchanges, at least in societies like ours, that are deemed exploitative seldom involve any constituted authority. Taxation may be a mode of exploitation, even a principal mode in certain forms of society, but exploitation cannot be assimilated *in toto* to taxation.

Apparently, the only model of unequal exchange that will

work, at least plausibly, is robbery.* But since robbery is unlawful, as well as unjust, since it threatens the very order market society depends upon, assimilating exploitation to robbery must appear wildly overstated, for many liberal writers. Thus wherever possible, many liberals prefer to overlook exploitation altogether, rather than construe it away. In either case, the very idea of voluntary, exploitative exchange—of ordinary market transactions that are exploitative—is virtually unthinkable. If exploitation is overlooked, then there can be no question of voluntary, exploitative exchange. And the result is the same if exploitation is assimilated to robbery: for the victim, robbery is always involuntary; the victim is unfree to fail to participate in the transaction.

Historically, notions of exploitation have come into prominence outside or at the peripheries of liberal social thought—in socialist literature and in classical and Marxian political economy. If, under the pervasive influence of liberal democratic theory, we are inclined to conjure exploitation away or to overlook it, then we would naturally conclude that most, if not all, charges of exploitation coming from these non- or marginally liberal democratic sources—even if just in their intent—are incorrectly and misleadingly formulated. To talk of exploitation, and particularly of voluntary exchanges that are exploitative, it might then seem, is to accede, eclectically and inadmissibly, to forms of discourse about social reality that are confused and misleading. Would it not be better, many might think, just to drop talk of exploitation altogether?

Voluntary or consensual exchange seems the very model of a legitimate transfer. But why should consent confer legitimacy? That consent does confer legitimacy has become so common-

---

*Characteristically, liberal writers fail to countenance even putative cases of exploitation, and therefore have no need to assimilate such cases to robbery (or anything else). It is on the margins of the dominant tradition, among critics of the existing order, that this move is sometimes attempted. Thus for some socialists, who consider the wage bargain an exploitative exchange, profit is theft.

sensical, so deeply entrenched, that an answer does not even seem warranted. However this intuition is not quite so unproblematic as first appears, and is, moreover, very likely historically peculiar to societies where market relations predominate.

Even the most ardent proponents of consentual transactions realize that there are at least some exchanges that cannot rightfully be concluded, even if all interested parties (voluntarily) consent. When consentual arrangements clash with legal prohibitions, normally the legal prohibitions take precedence. Thus where minimum wage laws are in force, one cannot contract to work for less than the minimum wage. Very often, the rationale for such prohibitions will appeal to the public interest, suggesting that the otherwise legitimate transaction must be overriden for considerations of welfare. But non-welfare considerations might also be invoked. One might appeal, for example, to real or potential harm to third parties, or even, as in the case of proscribed "victimless crimes" such as prostitution, to an offended public morality. Many prohibitions of consentual transactions may well be illiberal, according to the prevailing acceptance of the term, but they do enjoy at least legal priority over consentual arrangements in liberal democratic polities, whenever they are, for better or worse, in force. In earlier times, most restrictions on consentual arrangements were customary or traditional, rather than strictly legal. Until relatively recently, restrictions of this sort governed many economic and social activities that today are regulated through markets. It would seem that where the scope of consentual exchange is severely restricted, whether by law or custom, it would be less than obvious, and perhaps even counter-intuitive (in many instances), to suppose that consent confers legitimacy. However where market relations predominate and are thought "natural," as in virtually all liberal democratic polities, consentual exchange does appear at least presumptively legitimate. I would speculate, contrary to what is often supposed, that it is not our pre-social intuitions about the rightfulness of voluntary exchange that promote the extention of market relations, but the market relations themselves that bring about our sense of the legitimacy of consentual transfers.

Even if this causal connection is overstated, it is indisputable, I think, that our intuitions concerning the legitimacy of voluntary exchange are, to some very large extent, historically relative, and have much to do with the existence and prevalence of markets. It is to these intuitions we must now turn, shifting the focus from voluntary exchanges as such, to voluntary exchanges in markets. This shift is appropriate, in order eventually to consider exploitative exchange. For it is, after all, primarily in attacks on the market, as a mechanism for allocating resources and distributing social wealth, that the notion of exploitation has intruded upon liberal discourse. Is this intrusion warranted?

The Voluntary and the Free

Intuitively market transactions seem entirely proper and legitimate because the transacting parties have freedom of choice. By definition, market transactions are voluntary, no one is unfree either to enter or fail to enter into the transaction in virtue of the interference of anyone else. But an exchange may be voluntary, it seems, without the transacting parties having what might be called *full* freedom of choice: for there may not be a sufficiently significant choice set from among which to choose. Full freedom of choice, let us say, requires both that exchanges be voluntary and that there is a significant range of alternatives in contention. This is one reason why, traditionally, the mere existence of markets is not generally deemed sufficient for freedom of choice. There must be *competitive* markets.*

The paradigmatically competitive market is that which reg-

*It should be noted that the case for competitive markets, in the main, appeals more to welfare consideration than to freedom. The existence of competitive markets (where economic agents are "price takers," unable by their own efforts to determine the prices of commodities) is a necessary condition for demonstrating the (Pareto) optimality of market allocations. Nonetheless, for those who do defend markets on libertarian grounds, the claim just asserted—that markets can be competitive—is, or at least ought to be, a stipulation.

ulates exchange in "the early and rude state of society," imagined by Adam Smith and used, as an analytic model (and sometimes as a historical hypothesis) throughout classical political economy. Here each person or household owns his own means of production, and the products of labor that are not directly consumed (by their immediate producers) are exchanged in voluntary (market) transactions. Such market arrangements are plainly competitive; there are many producers and, consequently, many options from among which to choose. No particular choice is favored, as it were, by the choice situation. More important, it is not even inevitable that some exchange or other take place. By hypothesis, each producing unit is relatively self-sufficient; and production is largely for use rather than exchange. In consequence, individuals or households might choose simply not to exchange the products of their labor. It is noteworthy that what motivates exchange, for Smith, is not such much need, as a *psychological* "propensity to truck, barter and exchange." The social context is neutral; it is entirely non-constraining with respect to exchanges. For an external observer, entirely ignorant of the particular proclivities of an economic agent (beyond the general propensity to truck, barter and exchange), it would be impossible, in this view, to predict the agent's transactions. The probability of choosing any particular option, or even on a particular occasion of making no exchange at all, would be, so far as the observer could tell, the same.

However where the products of labor are seldom, if ever, directly consumed, as under any system of production where the division of labor is well developed, self-sufficiency no longer pertains; and the option of making no exchange at all is, in most cases, practically foreclosed. Thus the *prima facie* legitimacy of market transactions in the early and rude state of society is already diminished. With capitalism, however, an even more telling deviation from the paradigm is introduced.

The key feature of the early and rude state of society is the stipulation that each producing unit owns the means of production it uses in the production process. Under capitalism, on the contrary, the means of production are not owned by the direct producers, but by a class of non-producers. In the early and rude state of society what exchanges are (some) products of labor. But under capitalism the direct producers have no products of labor to exchange; the products of labor are *owned* by those who own the means of production with which the direct producers work. The direct producers, then, can exchange only their labor or, more strictly, their labor power (as Marxists would say): their capacity to produce products of labor. Thus the institution of capitalist social relations (free wage labor, ownership of the means of production and therefore of the product of labor by a class of non-producers) extends the scope of market transactions from products of labor exclusively to products of labor *and* labor power itself. The impetus to exchange products of labor is, we have seen, greater under capitalism than in the early and rude state of society, if only in virtue of an expanded division of labor, but the impetus to exchange labor power for sustenance, for those who have nothing else to exchange, is virtually irresistible. Even where there is a sellers' market in labor power, so that the choice of any particular employer is relatively unconstrained, the direct producer is still effectively constrained to exchanged labor power to some employer or other in return for a wage. Under capitalism, then, direct producers enter into the wage bargain not at all because of a psychological propensity to truck, barter and exchange, but because they are without property.*

Nonetheless, the worker's exchange of labor power for a wage is still, strictly, voluntary. There is no one with respect to whom the worker is unfree not to enter into the exchange. Still he does not have that full freedom of choice that, according to our considered intuitions, guarantees the legitimacy of consensual transfers. The distinction between voluntary and fully free exchange is plausibly overlooked in the early and rude state of society.

*The capitalist too is moved less by a propensity to truck, barter and exchange than by the need to accumulate capital. The capitalist who does not accumlate does not long survive (as a capitalist), given the dynamics of the capitalist system. Survival as a capitalist may be less urgent than bare survival, but it is nonetheless an imposed need, constraining the capitalist's choices.

Under capitalism, however, the distinction becomes especially pertinent. For even if we overlook the historically relative character of our views about the legitimacy of market transactions, our sense of the legitimacy of market transactions under capitalism (particularly the wage bargain) rests on what we now see to be an unwarranted identification of capitalist markets (as faced by direct producers) with markets in the early and rude state of society. This confusion pervades a good deal of thinking about the legitimacy of market transactions. It is important to investigate what accounts for it.

Abstractness

A voluntary exchange is one that is not unfree, that is unconstrained by others. To be unconstrained by others is generally understood to mean unconstrained by the *deliberate* activity of others (see chapter 2): A is rendered unfree by B to do X, only if B intends to prevent A from doing X. If A is prevented from doing X by some sort of institutional impediment, so long as there is no deliberate contrivance of this impediment by persons with a view to preventing A, or persons like A, from doing X, A is not unfree to do X. Thus where there exists a capitalist market in labor power, if A is a direct producer without control (ownership) of the means of production, he is unable, but not unfree, say, to start his own factory. We have seen that this stipulation is at least somewhat counter-intuitive and also that it is not, strictly, part of the core theory. On the other hand, we know it does have advantages—for sorting cases out neatly and unambiguously and for making room for social ideals—like justice or equality—that are conceptually distinct from freedom (see chapter 2).

But whatever the conceptual advantages, it is plain that when we construe matters this way, the price paid is a complete abstraction of institutional arrangements from considerations of freedom and unfreedom. The worker's exchange of labor power for a wage under capitalism and the relatively self-sufficient farmer's exchange of, say, a bushel of wheat for a bushel of corn in the early and rude state of society are depicted alike. One looks no further than the transaction itself. Each is a voluntary exchange; each, therefore, is equally legitimate, equally free. That the worker has no choice but to exchange labor power for a wage (from some employer or other), while the farmer could just as well consume wheat instead of corn, does not matter. These differences are ignored or, rather, abstracted from. The exchange itself is what counts—not its setting.

This abstractness is hardly innocent: it introduces a clear bias with respect to forms of institutions. What should be avoided, so far as possible, are institutional arrangements concocted to prevent or inhibit voluntary transactions, and what should be encouraged are institutions that extend the scope of voluntary exchange. That the outcome of such transactions may in fact diminish an individual's ability to do what he wants—thereby, it would seem, diminishing his freedom—is of no account; what alone matters is to retract the scope of unfreedom relations. Thus the characteristic abstractness of liberal (and liberal democratic) theory introduces a bias for markets: for voluntary, bilateral exchanges.

Of course this bias cannot extend to anarchism, as a way of eliminating all restrictions on markets, because states are needed to support markets. However grudgingly, even the most "libertarian" liberals concede the need for a coercive order to regulate market behavior. Markets flourish not in splendid anarchy, but in societies regulated by states, states that specify and enforce a framework within which market transactions occur.

But wherever market relations are implemented, they cannot be faulted for restricting liberty: so far as freedom is in question, they are beyond reproach. Moves away from markets are always restrictions on liberty. In pre- or non-market societies, this kind of tendential bias is, of course, profoundly unsettling for the existing order. The apparently innocent conflation of voluntary and fully free exchange becomes a call to implement and expand market relations. And this call, in concrete historical circumstances, is tantamount to a call for capitalism, the most viable form of market society. However where capitalist market relations already exist, this bias turns into a call for their conservation. We cannot be more free than in markets. The task, then, is vigilantly to preserve what we have.

Thus the market appears "natural," both in the sense that it is the institutional form proper to our nature as free human beings and, more importantly, in the sense that whatever constrains economic agents where market relations pertain is conceptually of a piece with the constraints of bare nature. These impediments are simply given. The underlying institutional setting of market transactions therefore falls outside the scope of criticism, at least so far as freedom is the overwhelmingly most important consideration in assessing social and political arrangements. If transactions are voluntary, but in some palpable sense unjust, as are those exchanges deemed exploitative, even if the injustice is acknowledged, it is held to be, at most, of only minor importance in assessing social arrangements. More often, the injustice simply goes unacknowledged. So farreaching is the liberal's concern that transactions be voluntary, that the settings in which voluntary transactions occur generally avoid scrutiny on any grounds whatsoever. It is only when the pattern of "natural" arrangements is violated, by expressly coercive or otherwise "deviant" intervention, as in robbery, that social relations of differential power become relevant for assessing the legitimacy of transactions.

Thus the unwarranted conflation of voluntary and fully free exchange, the basis for the general reluctance liberal writers exhibit to countenance exploitation, rests, ultimately, on the abstractness of liberal theory, its insensitivity to institutional settings, and its consequent bias for markets and against whatever restricts the scope of market arrangements.

Exploitation

Exploitation is problematic for the dominant tradition in virtue of a defect of that tradition: its abstractness and the consequences of this abstractness for the liberal democratic view of freedom.

Liberal democratic theory provides no good reason for rejecting the concept of exploitation, and therefore no good reason for overlooking what many take to be the injustice of the wage bargain and other market transactions. Are we , then, entitled to include the concept of exploitation—and of voluntary, exploitative exchange—in the conceptual apparatus we use for assessing social arrangements? And if so, can it somehow be incorporated into liberal democratic theory?

We could, of course, establish the concept of exploitation by pointing out an instance. We know that any plausible candidate will be an unequal exchange in which at least one of the parties is not fully free, even in the manner of the early and rude state of society, but is instead constrained by social relations of unequal power. As just indicated, and in line with the history of the concept, it seems that the wage bargain is a prime candidate for the title of voluntary, exploitative exchange. Is this the case?

The wage bargain is, of course, motivated by unequal power relations. Moreover, it is strictly voluntary (unlike robbery), even if it is not fully free. If the wage bargain is to count as a voluntary, exploitative exchange, one further condition must be satisfied; it must result in a net transfer of value to the stronger party.

It should be noted that, for Marx, whose account of exploitation is surely of the greatest historical and conceptual importance, this latest condition is not unequivocally satisfied. In opposition to the classical economists, Marx insisted that in the process of appropriating "surplus value," labor power typically exchanges *at its value.* For Marx, then, the wage bargain is an exchange of equals, and not, as it would seem, a net transfer of value to the stronger party. Of course, in Marx's view, there are other senses in which this exchange manifestly is unfavorable to the worker: in *Capital* and elsewhere, Marx speaks eloquently of the human degradation that follows in its wake. And even in strictly economic terms, the wage bargain is, in Marx's account, a component in the process of exploitation *at the level of production:* a process that does result, ultimately, in a net transfer of value to the stronger party—and in a manifestly unequal and un-

just distribution of social wealth. In these senses, the wage bargain, even for Marx, is an unequal exchange—even if it is, literally, an exchange of equals.

If Marx is right, it is misleading, and strictly incorrect, to focus on exploitation at the level of exchange. Exploitation, strictly speaking, does not occur at the point of the wage bargain, but in the production process itself. It is intrinsic to the economic structure or "mode of production." Profit is therefore not, strictly, a deduction from wages, a transfer from workers to capitalists. In contrast to some classical and also to some contemporary neo-Ricardian positions, capitalist exploitation, in Marx's view, is not a result of a struggle, overt or implicit, between capital and labor for the distribution of social wealth. It is instead a result—under prevailing social relations—of the process of producing social wealth. For Marx, then, it verges on a category mistake, albeit a suggestive one, to describe the wage bargain as a voluntary, exploitative exchange.

Whatever finally is made of the concept of exploitation, it is clear that liberal democratic theory need not exclude it. Assessments of its viability and adequacy depend on a variety of considerations, including developments within economic theory. Pending good and unexpected reasons to the contrary, there is no point in denying the reality of exploitation. Neither is there any good reason to assimilate away its concept, as those liberal democrats who do recognize exploitation are inclined to do. If voluntary, exploitative exchange is ultimately unacceptable, it will not be for liberal reasons.

It is one thing to determine whether or not an exchange is voluntary, and quite another to determine whether or not it is exploitative. That liberals attend to the former and generally neglect the latter determination is unnecessary, but not surprising in a tradition where the principal, if not the only, pertinent determination in assessing transactions seems to be whether or not exchanges are strictly voluntary; that is, whether or not unfreedom relations pertain. The political bearing of this tendency to oppose unfreedom with an undifferentiated notion of freedom has already been indicated: it is a condition for the liberal case for capitalist markets. So important—and pervasive—is this tendency, therefore, that it bears further scrutiny.

Degrees of Freedom

It is striking that liberal democrats tend to oppose freedom and unfreedom as starkly as they do. This opposition is achieved, we have seen, by effectively conflating the (fully) free and the voluntary. But what motivates this move? It is as though liberals were constitutionally incapable of asking what is plainly a question of great relevance, even from their own standpoint: the question "how much freedom is there?" Surely, if pushed, liberal democrats would admit that in the absence of unfreedom relations, individuals may be more or less free, that there are different degrees, so to speak, of freedom. The question how free an individual is to do X is plainly an intelligible question. And it is an important question. It must be addressed if we are to determine, in general, how free an individual is, and therefore, where societies are viewed as collections of individuals, how free different societies are. To avoid asking how much freedom there is is tantamount to foreclosing the attempt to assess social arrangements with respect to degrees or levels of freedom. And liberal democrats have no good reason to forbear from attempting such assessments.

In practice, of course, liberal democrats do not at all forbear from judging how free societies are. In holding, even if only implicitly, that the absence of unfreedom relations, is alone pertinent for assessements of this sort, liberal theory is, we have seen, biased in favor of markets and, therefore, in this historical epoch, in favor of capitalism. That capitalist markets may severely diminish some or even most individuals' opportunities for doing what they want—thus (plausibly) diminishing their freedom without rendering them, strictly, unfree—is apparently of no account. It seems, in short, that liberal democrats' judgments about how free societies are, typically, are incorrect. And needlessly incorrect.

For there is nothing in the core theory, or so it seems, that requires abstracting the institutional context away. The abstractness of liberal democratic theory, so far as it supports conflating voluntary and fully free exchange, would seem entirely eliminable.

However, the issue is a bit more complicated. To see how, it will be well to speculate, provisionally, how liberals might go about determining how free an agent is, were they to attempt to do so. In reflecting on this question, the precarious character of the liberal democrat's commitment to freedom for its own sake is brought into question, and the role of liberal democratic theory's characteristic abstractness—illustrated so perspicuously by its treatment of exploitation and its effective denial of voluntary, exploitative exchange—is put into focus.

Unfreedom is a social relation, logically independent of any sense of frustrated desire on the part of those who are unfree, and freedom too, as the opposite of unfreedom, is likewise independent of desire (see chapter 2). An agent is free with respect to specifiable others to do X, whether or not he wants to do X. However if we are to address the question of the degree or extent of freedom within a liberal democratic framework, desire must be taken into account. More precisely, what must be considered is the *value* of alternative courses of action available to an agent, where, as throughout liberal democratic theory, value is construed as a want-regarding, not ideal-regarding, notion.[3]

Want-independent aspects of choice situations seem only minimally and indirectly related to determining how free an agent is. Thus the physical properties of alternative options have no immediate bearing on the extent of a person's freedom, except insofar as they determine, or figure in the determination of, what an individual's wants are. Likewise, a person is not more or less free just because he has more or fewer choices, where choices are individuated according to some value-neutral principle. Are we more free, say, to satisfy a thirst if we have a choice from among ten brands of rose hips tea or if we have a smaller choice-set, consisting of one type of each tea, coffee and beer? Undoubtedly, under most circumstances (but not in all, as we shall see momentarily), it would be granted we are freer in the latter case, though the number of choices is greater in the former. What matters, then, is plainly not the number of options, but their range. In assessing the extent of freedom, the relevant consideration is the degree of qualitative difference pertaining between available options, not the sheer number of choices available.

And these qualitative differences are not, so to speak, in the options themselves. They are not physical differences. Rather, what matters is just our evaluations of the available choices. The range of options available to a person is determined, ultimately, by his interests; or since interests are reducible to wants, by a person's wants or desires. Thus it is conceivable, though quite unlikely, that an individual might be more free with ten or even two brands of rose hips tea and nothing else. Then, for this individual, the range of options is greater the more choices of rose hips tea he has, all other options being irrelevant. The situation is, of course, highly improbable, but it cannot be ruled out. For what matters in assessing the extent of a person's freedom is his interests, and, in the liberal democratic view, interests, as we know, are substantively unconstrained.

How free a person is, then, depends not on the choices he actually confronts, but on his evaluation of these choices. In the final analysis, assessments of freedom, whether for individuals or for societies (collections of individuals), are relative to these individuals' ends and therefore, ultimately, to their wants or desires.

Where the extent or degree of freedom is taken into account, then, desire enters into the liberal view of freedom in a way liberals can ill abide. The independence of the liberal component is jeopardized, it seems, if freedom, like interest, is thought to have desire at its core. For it would be difficult in such circumstances to maintain freedom as an end-in-itself, and to resist the temptation to construe freedom instrumentally, as a means for advancing individuals' interests. It is worth recalling that in On Liberty Mill sometimes represented himself as having succumbed to this temptation (which he, of course, took to be an advantage), presenting what he claimed to be a utilitarian justification for liberty. But

liberals generally, and even Mill some of the time, do value freedom in its own right, and so too do liberal democrats who *also*
value welfare as another, distinct end. To maintain the independence and coequal status of these values would seem arbitrary,
though, if desire enters into the constitution of both.

Thus the abstractness of liberal theory, in virtue of which
liberals focus just on the presence or absence of unfreedom relations and ignore degrees of freedom, does play a role of some
importance for liberal democratic theory. It helps to maintain a
sense of the autonomy and integrity of the liberal component, its
conceptual independence within the liberal democratic project.
This is not to say that liberalism would collapse into welfareism,
were we to countenance degrees of freedom. The point is just that
any subordination of freedom to welfare, or even the hint of same,
is anathema to the spirit, if not the letter, of liberal democratic
theory. We have seen how in order to salvage the liberal democratic project, liberal democrats are willing—and even eager—effectively to jettison the democratic component, and thus to
sacrifice welfare for liberty (see chapter 8). To countenance talk
of degrees of freedom threatens to have a contrary effect, in marked
opposition to the tendency of liberal democratic politics. Liberal
democrats effectively meet that threat by evading it, avoiding the
issue of degrees of freedom.

Still, nothing in the core theory entails a strict opposition of
freedom and unfreedom; one could, therefore, retain liberal democratic notions of freedom and interest, while taking account of
the degree of freedom individuals (and societies) enjoy. To do so
would doubtless drive a wedge into the close association of liberal
democracy and capitalism—as does allowing talk of exploitation
and voluntary, exploitative exchange—but these counters to liberal democracy's historical position are not ruled out by the core
theory. Again, what is jeopardized is just our sense of the integrity
of the liberal component. It seems, then, that the cost of taking
too bold a stand against liberal democracy's characteristic abstractness is to strain both the objectives of liberal democratic
theory (articulating independent liberal and democratic judg-

ments on political institutions) and the thrust of liberal democratic politics (subordinating democracy to liberalism). However this may be, the possibility of a revisionist liberalism is, as matters now stand, still quite alive. I will return to this question more directly in chapter 10.

Theory and Practice

It should be stressed, finally, that the abstractness of liberal democratic theory does not by itself account for the appropriateness of the charge very often, and very justly, leveled against existing liberal democratic polities: that in their actual functioning, particular interests (specifically those wielding great economic power within a capitalist economy) wield political power as well, even in voting situations, far beyond their numbers. Needless to say, any deviation from the letter and the spirit of the principle that all count equally in the determination of the social choice is in blatant violation of liberal democracy's theoretical pretensions, and should be deplored by liberal democrats, so long as their commitment is in fact to liberal democratic theory and not, come what may, to the status quo.

Pointing out a gap between the theory and practice of liberal democracy by itself settles nothing. Ultimately, whatever gaps there are must be accounted for, and their implications drawn out. What is at issue, most generally, is the complex question of the connection between liberal democratic theory and the institutions through which it is implemented. This general theme was broached in chapter 8 in connection with representative government. I would speculate, beyond the conclusions reached there, that a gap between the theory and practice of liberal democracy is crucial for the continued functioning of liberal democratic institutions generally, and that liberal democratic theory facilitates the effective betrayal of its theoretical pretensions by making the real power relations that support liberal democratic politics and its institutions, thereby helping to legitimate this politics and these institutions. But to sustain such a position requires considerations that go far beyond the scope of the present study. The concern here is not immediately with "the real world of liberal democracy," to borrow an expression of C. B. Macpherson's, but with its theory, and with the real world only to the extent that it impinges on the theory. To investigate the real world of liberal democracy and the role of liberal democratic theory in that world would require concrete historical investigation of actual liberal democratic polities and institutions. It is hoped that the present study will encourage such investigations, and that this critique of liberal democracy's theory will, to some degree, facilitate them. But it hardly stands in their place.

This is not the occasion, then, to reflect on the significance of the overwhelming fact that liberal democratic states and institutions fail miserably to live up to their theoretical pretensions. What is at issue here is the character of those pretensions, whether they are realized by existing institutional arrangements or not. It is with this concern in mind that we turn, finally, to consider the prospects for reforming liberal democratic theory, so to speak, from within. Here again, as we shall see, the real world—as evidenced in ongoing political currents—impinges on the theory.

10 / Beyond Liberal Democracy?

LIBERAL democracy's core theory articulates liberal and democratic (aggregative welfare), but not distributional, judgments on political institutions. Thus its vision of proper political arrangements ignores considerations of justice (fairness) in the distribution of benefits and burdens, and considerations of equality as well, except of course in the distribution of liberty and the determination of collective choices. The damaging abstractness of liberal democratic theory is, it seems, at least in part a consequence of this neglect. Arguably also liberal democracy's unacknowledged, but effective, negation of its democratic component in representative government and the institutions surrounding it would be less easily achieved if liberal democracy's political theory took distributional considerations squarely into account. Taking justice seriously might well be a boon for democracy. And taking justice seriously would surely also help to counteract liberal democratic theory's increasingly evident irrelevance to so much of contemporary political life, where the ongoing functioning of liberal democratic states, and the experience of people living in them, have brought considerations of justice and equality increasingly to the fore.

Contemporary political writers do, of course, address distributional questions, but not usually in the context of an explicitly political theory. Rigorously respecting classical liberalism's distinction of the social from the political, it has become fashionable, while tacitly retaining loyalty to liberal democratic political theory, to uphold justice as "the first virtue of *social* institutions,"[1] thus salvaging for society what is excluded from politics. Focusing on justice this way plainly will not undo the theoretical defects already pointed out for liberal democratic *political* theory: its abstractness, the likely incoherence of simultaneously articulating liberal and democratic judgments on political institutions, the peculiarity and apparent untenability of some of its most basic assumptions. But supplementing liberal democratic theory with a theory of justice may go far in remedying liberal democratic theory's apparent shortcomings as a normative vision, its failure to articulate all that we might suppose should be expresed in an adequate vision of a good society.

In the introduction, I called programs for supplementing liberal democratic theory with a theory of justice, *social democratic theories*. (The appropriateness of this designation will become clear by the end of this chapter.) There is, I think, an immediately political reason motivating contemporary social democratic theory. Within actual liberal democracies, in part thanks to liberal democracy's links with capitalism, there generally are vastly unequal, and almost certainly unjust, distributions of social wealth and hence of societal benefits and burdens. It is in large measure to counter these inequalities and injustices that welfare state policies have been implemented in varying degrees in virtually all liberal democracies. I would hazard that attempts such as Rawls' to center moral philosophy around a theory of justice are properly seen as theoretical representations of this strain of contemporary liberal democratic politics. The express intent of welfare state measures is to render liberal democracies more just.* A moral philosophy that puts justice at the center of its concerns, while retaining conceptual affinity to classical liberal democratic theory, gives theoretical expression to this strain of ongoing Western political practice.

But except in remedying its vision of a good society, making justice central will not help liberal democratic theory as such. The

---

*It goes without saying, however, that no simple identification should be drawn between what defenders of welfare state measures claim on their behalf and their actual functioning in existing states. The theory of the welfare state, in its actual functioning, is an urgent matter for concrete historical and empirical investigation.

theoretical problems noted above remain, even if liberal democratic political theory is subordinated effectively to a theory of
justice, just as the state itself is subordinated to society. Liberal
democratic theory is not merely inadequate as a vision; it is theoretically defective. What must be considered, finally, is whether
these defects are remediable. Can there be a political theory, conceptually continuous with the core theory, yet free from its more
objectionable theoretical features, as well as from the defects of
its normative vision?

The only sustained effort to date to develop an affirmative
answer to this question is, I believe, to be found in the writings
of C. B. Macpherson.[2] Macpherson does not represent his investigations in democratic theory quite in the terms just presented.
Even so, it is fair to construe much of what Macpherson does as
an attempt to develop an affirmative response; and there is, I think,
no more direct or illuminating way to explore this question than
by examination of Macpherson's positions.

Macpherson's intent is not just to correct liberal democratic
theory's vision along social democratic lines (though doing so is
a central concern of his). He aims to revise liberal democratic
theory as such. Much of what is to be gained by supplementing
liberal democratic theory with a theory of justice is in fact recu-
perated in Macpherson's proposed revisions of the dominant tradition. What is particularly radical and impressive is that Macpherson undertakes this task not by introducing considerations
from outside the domain of liberal democratic theory proper, but,
as it were, by redoing liberal democratic theory itself.

I will argue that the theoretical positions Macpherson elab-
orates and the continuity with liberal democratic theory he insists
upon are, in large measure, motivated politically. Macpherson's
efforts to remedy the failings of liberal democratic theory constitute a political intervention *within* political philosophy. To say
this is not at all to disparage what Macpherson develops, to depict
it as "ideology," rather than political philosophy. From *The Political Theory of Possessive Individualism* on, Macpherson has
amply and ably demonstrated the centrality of politics in the po-

litical thought of Hobbes and Locke and also of Bentham and Mill. Political philosophy, indeed, is nothing if it is not political. Thus if Macpherson's politics, like Hobbes' or Locke's or Bentham's or Mill's—or, for that matter, like Nozick's or Rawls'—is central to his thought, so far from indicating a philosophical lapse, a falling away from the standards appropriate for political philosophers, it is instead an indication, as with the giants of Western political theory—and influential contemporary political philosophers—of the range and honesty of his thought. For our purpose, this aspect of Macpherson's work is of central importance. In reading Macpherson politically, as he effectively forces us to do, the underlying political dimension of the issues explored here through Macpherson's work are brought into focus. It is my contention that, in the end, politics is decisive for determining whether an adequate political theory can indeed be developed out of, rather than apart from, liberal democratic theory.

Beyond Possessive Individualism

For many decades, Macpherson has waged a relentless campaign to expose and criticize what he calls "possessive individualist" assumptions running throughout the principal strains of Western political thought.* In developing a positive political philosophy, Macphersons's express intent is to "retrieve" what is of value in the liberal and democratic traditions, while breaking absolutely from the possessive individualist assumptions with which these traditions, on his view, are encumbered. According to Macpherson, what is wrong with possessive individualism is not so much conceptual as historical and even political. Possessive individu-

---

*In brief, the claim is that each person is the sole proprietor of his own person and capacities, and that each person has an infinite desire to appropriate resources (human, as well as natural). Society, then, becomes "a lot of free and equal individuals related to each other as proprietors of their own capacities and of what they have acquired by their exercise." See The Political Theory of Possessive Individualism, p.3 and, for a fuller account, pp. 263-64.

alist assumptions, Macpherson contends, have become historically outmoded. They are inadequate *for us—now*—because they
are no longer needed. In the early days of capitalism, according
to Macpherson, possessive individualist assumptions were crucial
for justifying institutions conducive to the development of a society's productive capacities and its store of wealth. Now, the
argument runs, productive capacities are sufficiently developed
and wealth sufficiently accumulated to render this "perverse,
artificial and temporary concept of man" obsolete.[3] However liberal democracy is not unsalvageable. In Macpherson's view, all
that is attractive in liberalism and democracy can be saved. *Democratic Theory*, the collection of essays where Macpherson provides the fullest account of his positive views, is appropriately
subtitled: *Essays in Retrieval.*

Thus it is Macpherson's express intent to continue liberal
democratic theory, but along new lines. His work does not constitute a break with liberal democratic theory, so much as an internal modification or, as the Hegelians would say, a "supercession" of it, in which the liberal component, while "negated" is
"incorporated." (Although Macpherson speaks at length of "democratic theory," in fact he has little to say about what I have called
the democratic component). Liberal democracy and its theory are,
in Macpherson's view, partially adequate. What is to come next
should incorporate that part which is adequate, while overcoming
the possessive individualism that continues to haunt the dominant
tradition. To develop such a theory is to go *beyond* liberal democratic theory, while remaining, so to speak, on the same terrain.

Macpherson's Division of Liberty

It will be convenient to concentrate on a polemical essay of Macpherson's entitled "Berlin's Division of Liberty,"[4] directed against
Isaiah Berlin's celebrated and influential "Two Concepts of Liberty."[5] Berlin's essay is, of course, among the most important recent contributions to orthodox liberalism; in writing against Ber-

lin, Macpherson confronts the tradition directly. In contention is the concept of freedom. In proposing a new "division of liberty" to counter Berlin's, Macpherson provides an example of what it is, in his view, to retain what is valuable in notions inherited from traditional liberalism, while rejecting what is outmoded and inadequate (possessive individualism), but still retaining continuity with the liberal democratic tradition.

Berlin distinguishes the liberal concept of freedom, which he calls "negative liberty," from its illiberal conterpart "positive liberty." Roughly, by negative liberty is meant the concept analysed here in chapter 2, while the term positive liberty designates the concept of freedom encountered most often in idealist political thought, described by both Berlin and Macpherson as "self-direction" or "self-mastery." Positive liberty, in Berlin's view, rests on inadequate conceptual foundations, but this is not all that is wrong with the concept. For Berlin, positive liberty is a dangerous notion, for it leads, intrinsically on his account, to the loss of negative liberty and *in extremis* to "totalitarian" usurpations of actual liberty in the name of a higher (but in fact unreal) freedom. Thus, for Berlin, the defense of negative liberty enjoins an all-out war on its adversary-counterpart "on grounds both of its liability to become an engine of oppression and of its embodying false assumptions about the human condition.[6]

This categorical rejection of positive liberty undercuts the proposal Macpherson advanced in "The Maximization of Democracy" and reiterated throughout his writings to base justifying theories on that strain in the dominant tradition that, according to Macpherson, coexists—uneasily—with the assumptions of possessive individualism: the strain that holds institutions justified to the extent they maximize "human powers."[7] For surely *freedom* to develop one's powers is just the kind of "self-mastery" Berlin attributes to positive liberty. The problem, then, is to rescue positive liberty, to retrieve its role in the maximization of powers, but to do so in a way that avoids what Berlin warns against—sanctioning the usurpation of real liberty in the name of "rational freedom." To this end, Macpherson proposes an alternative "division" of the concept of freedom.

For Macpherson, the rational freedom Berlin warns against is a debasement of positive liberty, not its inevitable outcome. This debasement is, in his account, largely a consequence of a conceptual mistake. It arises out of "a failure by theorists to see positive liberty in terms of the absence of impediments to man's developmental powers" and a corresponding failure, on the part of those holding political power, to deal with these impediments practically.[8] This, indeed, is Macpherson's principal reproach to orthodox liberalism. An adequate theory of liberty, he insists, cannot fail to take account of such impediments.

This is why the concept *negative liberty*, as Berlin formulates it, will not do. If a justifying theory based on the maximization of powers is to be developed, no account of freedom that fails to countenance impediments to the development of individuals' powers will be satisfactory. Thus the traditional liberal understanding of freedom, whether in Berlin's formulation or in traditional theory and practice, is unacceptable. In the traditional view, freedom is just the absence of unfreedom relations, where a person is unfree with respect to others only in virtue of their deliberate activities (see chapter 2). Thus institutional interferences, impediments of human contrivance, insofar as they do not arise out of explicit coercive intent, fall outside the scope of the concept of liberty. They are assimilated conceptually to natural impediments. We have seen, however, that this traditional view is not strictly enjoined by the core concept. The requirement that persons be free or unfree in virtue of the deliberate activity of others is, we know, not part of the core. And we have also seen (in chapter 9) how, albeit at some risk to the integrity of the liberal component, the core concept will admit consideration of degrees of freedom, and, to this extent, assessments of the impact of institutional arrangements on individuals' activities. I will consider shortly the extent to which these findings corroborate Macpherson's positions.

To be sure, neither Berlin nor any thoughtful liberal, no mat-

ter how faithful to the traditional understanding, is blind to the
detrimental effects of unintended, institutional impediments to
the exercise of liberty. The difference from Macpherson lies just
in how these impediments are to be understood. Berlin considers
them external to the concept, as *conditions* for the enjoyment of
liberty, and not as part of what is *meant* by liberty. It does not
seem that Macpherson anywhere objects to the cogency of this
move. Instead, characteristically, he attacks its underlying assumptions. Negative liberty, he insists, represents an unpardon-
able concession to possessive individualism.

It goes back through Bentham to Hobbes and beyond him to Galileo, from
whom Hobbes borrowed the concept of inertial motion: bodies, including
people, go on moving until they are stopped by the impact of other bodies.
This concept can properly be imported from mechanics into politics if,
and only if, one postulates, as Hobbes did, that every man's motion is
opposed and hindered by every other man's. That postulate in turn makes
good sense if, and only if, one is assuming an atomized market society
in which everyone is put on his own to compete with everyone for everything.[9]

In question here is not only possessive but also atomic individualism (see chapter 2). In this model, everyone's activity is
extrinsic to that of everyone else. The individual, construed as an
independent center of consciousness with antecendently given
desires, is the ultimate constituent of social reality.

The good for each person, in this view, is the satisfaction of
these antecendently given desires. Each "atom" pursues its own
"motion" until it is blocked by the motion of some other atom.
This blockage is unavoidable (indeed, universal is the case "where
everyone is put on his own to compete with everyone for everything"). But a good society will seek to minimize it. Institutional
arrangements *ought* to be such as to allow each atom, so far as
possible, the freedom to follow its own motion. This freedom is
negative liberty.

Macpherson deems this conception of persons and society
"limited" and "lacking in human dimension."[10] It fails to take
account of man as a social animal, of the fact that persons are not,

essentially, independent centers of consciousness, but social beings, depending essentially upon each other and upon society. To be sure, human nature is sufficiently plastic that a market society can go far to atomize social life and to turn persons into "atomic individuals." But even so, *intrinsic* social relations persist, at least sometimes, on the micro-level—in love, in the family, among close friends. In these and other arenas, at least sometimes, other persons are not just means for the satisfaction of antecedently given desires, but, in Kant's expression, ends-in-themselves. The point is to construct a society—or at least a theory of society— where such relations hold on the macro-level as well.

This, and not any sustained objection to Berlin's analysis of freedom, is the operative motivation underlying the development of the concept that Macpherson would have "supercede" negative liberty: *counter-extractive liberty.* In the essay "Problems of a Non-Market Theory of Democracy," Macpherson introduced the notion of *extractive power:* an extractive power is the ability to use other persons' capacities.[11]. The advantage of this concept, for Macpherson, is that it avoids picturing interference as "counter-inertial" and, therefore, always bad. Indeed, it acknowledges ungrudgingly that obstructions are necessary and seeks only to proscribe certain kinds—those that appropriate other individuals' powers extractively. Such interference, plainly, is an impediment to the free development of each person's own powers.

These extractive obstructions, according to Macpherson, arise out of ownership of capital and land. Thus the wage bargain is ruled out as are those other traditional economic liberties that define "free enterprise." These liberties, it is held, restrict freedom by giving rise to material impediments to the development of individuals' powers. The point, however, is to maximize powers, and thus to maximize freedom from such impediments. Therefore those material conditions that Berlin and other liberals would conceive apart from the concept of liberty (though, admittedly, important for its exercise) must be inscribed in the concept itself. This is what Macpherson attempts in formulating counter-extractive liberty.

The greatest possible freedom from material impediments is to be insured by providing equal access to the means of labor and life or, in other words, by eliminating extractive social relations. But would the elimination of extractive social relations actually achieve this end? In Macpherson's view, their elimination is at least necessary, if not by itself sufficient, for this end. But I would suggest that his assurances on this score, while firm, depend ultimately on a certain imprecision as to what counts as an extractive relation.

Suppose the traditional economic liberties were suspended: the wage bargain proscribed and private ownership of society's productive capacities eliminated. Material equality—equal access to the means of labor and life—would hardly result automatically. Instead, as Saint-Simon theorized for the society of the future, and as Engels speculated for a fully-achieved communist society, a considerable apparatus for "the administration of things and the direction of the process of production" would need to replace the market and the state, to coordinate individuals' activities. In redistributing resources initially and in maintaining this distribution subsequently, some persons, of course, would appropriate the product of others. This appropriation, to be sure, would not take place through private market transactions, but it would take place nonetheless—through the operation of a coercive political authority, the state (if, pace Marx, we allow the continued existence of states in such circumstances) or whatever comes to replace the state. There would be a massive and continual transfer of powers. Are these continual net transfers extractive? Macpherson appears to think not, presumably on the grounds that no one benefits in virtue of ownership. But as historical experience attests, individuals do not need to own resources juridically to benefit differentially from their use. It is enough to think of social systems such as those in eastern Europe or in the Soviet Union, where some individuals benefit exorbitantly from net transfers of the kind Macpherson seems to propose, but where the state, not those individuals, owns productive capital and land. At the very least, a more careful distinction between private ownership and its juridical form needs to be developed before Macpherson's position can be considered even plausible. The mere absence of legal ownership plainly counts for very little. But in any case, it is far from clear that material equality of the requisite sort can be achieved and maintained non-extractively.

It is worth recalling that the elimination of extractive social relations and even equal freedom from material impediments can be achieved through the market, at least in principle. Consider Adam Smith's early and rude state of society, considered by Macpherson in *The Political Theory of Possessive Individualism* as the "simple market society" model. In simple market societies, products of labor exchange as commodities, but everyone owns his own means of production and there is no market in labor (power). Significantly, this is just the economic structure Rousseau advised for the just state. The state could exist, Rousseau thought, only in the framework of a society of small, indepedent producers (predominantly rural, with "no one so rich as to be able to buy another and none so poor as to have to sell himself").[12] Material equality, at least within these limits, could only be achieved, Rousseau thought, by this type of political economic arrangement, and without material equality, he argued, the institutions of the just state cannot endure. But, as Rousseau realized, this political economic program is deeply problematic. Simple market societies are, by hypothesis, non-extractive and they do insure substantial material equality. But simple market society is utopian in the sense that it is not historically viable. Simple market society is inherently unstable; for wherever there are markets, there is a tendency for wealth to concentrate in increasingly fewer hands until eventually the overwhelming majority is reduced to a propertyless proletariat, with nothing but labor power to exchange. This tendency can, of course, be counteracted—say, by massive state interference or by coercive public opinion—but apparently not in ways liberals—and particularly libertarian capitalists—could endorse. Here, again Rousseau's example is instructive. To insure the continuation of the simple market society he advocates, Rousseau advised continual state interference with public opinion and a strict prohibition on the formation of groups that mediate between the individual and the state. Obviously, these blatantly illiberal measures are the last thing Macpherson or any writer in the liberal tradition would want. Nonetheless, they do seem well advised, if the point is to insure the absence of extractive relations (in Macpherson's sense) and material equality in a market framework. Of course, Macpherson, unlike Rousseau, does not advocate market arrangements, and so it is perhaps unfair to suggest that the illiberal measures Rousseau advises might be what Macpherson would need to insure the perpetuation of non-extractive social relations. But what is Macpherson's alternative? How are non-extractive, non-market arrangements to be conceived? Once we grant that Macpherson's appeal to public, juridical ownership is inadequate, even as a necessary condition for eliminating extractive relations, it seems we are left without a clear answer to this question. Plainly, Macpherson's express sympathies for socialism—however conceived—point in the direction of an answer, but the entire burden of his political philosophy then rests on theorizing that answer satisfactorily.

The problem, in short, is to conceive of a way to coordinate individuals' behavior that is non-extractive and that, at the same time, guarantees a substantial measure of material equality (sufficient for maximizing individuals' powers). Until a satisfactory account of such arrangements is forthcoming, it will be wise, I think, to be skeptical about counter-extractive liberty. For it is far from clear that we can, finally, conceive of liberty (in a sense continuous with traditional liberalism) without also countenancing extractive social relations (in Macpherson's sense).

The deeper question raised by Macpherson's notion of counter-extractive liberty is just the connection between so-called economic liberties and liberty *tout court*. Throughout virtually all of liberalism's long history, economic liberties were held to be inextricably part of liberty itself, and this view persists among virtually all important liberal writers today, including of course Macpherson's express antagonist, Isaiah Berlin. It is precisely this aspect of the tradition that insists on the inseparability of economic liberty from liberty itself that Macpherson wants to deny. He wants to insist that liberals can defensibly prohibit "capitalist relations among consenting adults."* But can this traditional view be undone? I will return to this question below.

The proposed complement to counter-extractive liberty, in Macpherson's scheme, is *developmental liberty*. This concept is intended to capture at least one sense of positive liberty: "individual self-direction." This sense can be distinguished, Macpherson insists, from its "idealist or metaphysical rationalist transformation" according to which "liberty is coercion, by the fully rational or by those who have attained self-mastery, of all the rest; coercion by those who say they know the truth of all those who do not (yet) know it."[13] Berlin, Macpherson argues, confounds these senses, among others, and thereby gives up too much in insisting that positive liberty be expunged from liberal theory. Too much, that is, from the point of view of a revised liberalism, reconstructed around the claim that maximizing individuals' powers is the basis for justifying political institutions.[14]

Developmental liberty differs from counter-extractive liberty only in what it emphasizes. What is central in both concepts is the absence of impediments to the development of individuals' powers. Counter-extractive liberty emphasizes the *absence* of impediments; developmental liberty emphasizes the resulting *development* of powers. Thus Macpherson's division of liberty is not at all parallel to Berlin's. Berlin distinguishes two concepts of liberty in order to retain one at the expense of the other. Macpherson develops a single concept that in its two emphasized aspects cuts across some of what is intended by both negative and positive liberty. From negative liberty, Macpherson would retain all but economic freedom; from positive liberty, he would retain only individual self-direction. Thus Berlin and Macpherson agree that liberals traditionally include too much under the heading of

*The expression is Robert Nozick's.

freedom. But they disagree as to what they would exclude, and what they would retrieve.

The cogency of developmental liberty therefore depends on the viability of its counterpart-equivalent, counter-extractive liberty, a concept about which some doubt has already been raised. Before building on that doubt, though, it will be instructive to consider what developmental liberty seems to add to Macpherson's account of freedom.

Developmental liberty is posed in contradistinction to idealist conceptions of freedom according to which one may be "forced to be free," to do what (as a rational agent) one *really* wants, whether or not these real wants (rational desires) are known to the agent. Developmental liberty nonetheless is thought to retrieve part of what is intended by positive liberty. A historical link between positive liberty and non-Hobbesian, particularly idealist, notions of rational agency is both easy to document and to account for. It is leading idealists, from Rousseau through Hegel to such Hegelian liberals as T. H. Green and Bernard Bosanquet that Berlin has in mind in making the case against positive liberty. To purge liberalism of positive liberty is, in effect, to purge it of idealist influences. And this is as one would expect. Without some notion of rational desire of the sort idealists maintain, without some distinction between *Willkür* and *Wille* (Kant), between the private will and the general will (Rousseau), between empirical and rational willing, there is in fact no difference between freedom as the absence of particular forms of constraint (negative liberty) and freedom as self-direction or self-control (positive liberty). Where there is no rational as opposed to merely empirical willing, but just willing *simpliciter*, self-direction is just the absence of the appropriate constraints. Positive liberty, then, collapses into negative liberty.

This is precisely the problem with developmental liberty. If, as Macpherson plainly wants, the development of powers is unconstrained by the requirements of practical reason (on any non-Hobbesian view), if a person develops powers just by doing what he wants (where wants are taken as given and immune from rational criticism), developmental liberty passes into negative liberty or, more strictly, into the concept Macpherson would have supercede negative liberty, counter-extractive liberty. Thus developmental liberty retrieves an aspect of positive liberty only in the palest of senses: instead of full-fledged self-direction or self-control, we are left just with independence from others. Without a notion of rational desire or its functional equivalent, the outcome could hardly be otherwise. I have already suggested that rational desire cannot be accommodated within an essentially Hobbesian view of rational agency, and that attempts to develop a theory of rational desire from such a foundation, including Rawls' theory of primary goods, therefore fail (see chapter 2). If this suggestion is right, the only hope is to find a functional equivalent for rational desire. The problem is analogous to that faced by traditional liberal democrats who would ascribe egoistic motives to Hobbesian rational agents (see chapter 4).* Since for Hobbesians and liberal democrats, reason is perfectly agnostic with respect to the ends persons hold, permitting altruistic or social ends as well as egoistic ones, the claim for egoism can only rest on assumptions about human nature—that persons are in fact egoists rather than altruists or social beings. Macpherson too appeals finally to human nature. Developmental liberty does what Macpherson intends because he thinks persons have the right sorts of inclinations: to value productive labor over acquisitiveness and cooperation over competition. Thus if persons are by nature sociable and solidary, there is no need for a practical reason that enjoins a "harmony of rational wills" such as Kant envisioned for "the kingdom of ends." The desired harmony follows from our human, not our rational nature. Thus just as acquisitve nature

---

*We might, for present purposes, speak of possessive individualist rather than egoistic motives, but, strictly speaking, these notions are not quite the same. Possessive individualism is a view of society, as well as of the individuals who constitute society; it incorporates atomic individualism and also the notion that persons are proprietors of themselves. Possessive individualists are egoists; but it is possible to uphold egoism without maintaining all that is included by Macpherson under possessive individualism. For now, the weaker, exclusively psychological notion of egoism is sufficient.

(roughly, Macpherson's possessive individualism) finally enters liberal democratic theory via psychology, so too, for Macpherson, possessive individualism is overcome and a quite different picture of humankind and human society takes its place in virtue of a different psychology.

Again, this recourse to psychology in no way violates liberal democracy's core theory. The core is strictly neutral with respect to assumptions about human nature, however much its view of rational agency may suggest egoism. In principle, the core theory can accommodate what Macpherson proposes, just as it traditionally has accommodated possessive individualism. It may be that Macpherson relies on an overly sanguine view of human potentialities. But then the more traditional view could be faulted for its pessimism. The fact that people in liberal societies do generally conform to the possessive individualist model is of little consequence once we admit, as Macpherson plainly assumes, that what acquisitiveness there is in human beings is more a product of market relation than an eternal truth to which markets conform. Empirical evidence is undoubtedly decisive for adjudicating competing human nature claims. But which way, if any, the available evidence inclines is anything but clear. Thus Macpherson's speculations are as much in order as are the more traditional views. For Hobbes and traditional liberal democrats, individuals seek to maximize egoistic values in accordance with their acquisitive natures. For Macpherson, they seek to develop powers in a spirit of harmony and social solidarity and mutual respect for each other (as bearers of powers). Hobbesian and Macphersonian individuals have different values and therefore different preference orderings—but for both Hobbes and Macpherson, the point, in the end, is just to maximize over those orderings individuals have. The difference, in short, is in the (partial) account traditional and Macphersonian liberals respectively give of individuals' wants.

This difference is no doubt of great importance. But it hardly suffices for capturing the idealist notion of freedom as autonomy, nor for adding anything to what is left of negative liberty, once the traditional economic freedoms are excised. For there simply is no division between counter-extractive and developmental liberty. If talk of developmental liberty adds anything to Macpherson's account, it is by focusing on his view of human nature, a view radically at odds with that of the tradition with which he seeks to retain continuity. From that tradition, however, Macpherson has stricken the economic liberties. We now turn to the warrant for this move. Can political and economic liberties be divided?

Continuity

Where, as throughout liberal theory, unfreedom is counterposed to an undifferentiated freedom, the place of the economic liberties is virtually assured. Since economic liberites emphatically are liberties, according to the liberal's notion of freedom, their retraction or, worse, their proscription plainly diminishes total freedom. If the point is to maximize freedom, as liberal democrats want, the economic freedoms must therefore be retained. No wedge can be driven between these liberties and others. Thus the market becomes the primal liberal institution (see chapter 9).

However where degrees of freedom are taken into account—as liberal democracy's core theory, if not its traditional practice, allows—the propriety of dividing off the economic liberties becomes an open question. Then for liberals to divide and then expunge economic from other liberties, they would have to show that the existence of these liberties has the effect of diminishing total liberty. Moves away from markets increase the number and extent of unfreedom relations. Would this retraction of liberty be offset by a gain in total liberty?

The point is not, at least immediately, to argue that social welfare in general gains when economic liberties are proscribed. Neither is the point to argue, as Macpherson comes perilously close to doing, on perfectionist grounds—that individuals become better (their powers more developed) when economic liberties are proscribed.[15] The calculation, such as it is, is to be drawn solely with reference to freedom. Otherwise, liberal democrats would find themselves committed to the view that liberty can be traded off for increases in welfare (or even worse: for perfectionist reasons). Such trade-offs, we know, violate a fundamental intent of liberal democratic theory. There can be no substantive liberal component, if liberty can be traded off for other values.

Macpherson, in the main, does argue in the way just described. He insists, in effect, that capitalist market relations tend in general to thwart developmental liberty and thereby to diminish total liberty. The great majority who do not own property in the means of production are, Macpherson insists, substantially less free than they might otherwise be under non-market (socialist) arrangements; they are less free to develop their powers. And this loss is in no way offset by the greater freedom of those who do hold productive property.* Therefore, in the final reckoning, freedom is best served by restricting—indeed, eliminating—the traditional economic liberties.

If I am right in holding that developmental liberty adds nothing to Macpherson's account of freedom, this argument would be better restated without express reference to that concept. Then the point would be just that in proscribing the economic liberties, in general we render persons more free to do what they want. If Macpherson is right about human nature, what people will in general want to do is develop their powers. If human nature is not as Macpherson supposes, people will undertake to realize less lofty objectives. But, in any case, the argument runs, eliminating capitalist markets—the institutional form of economic liberty—augments total liberty.

Plainly this question cannot be settled definitively *a priori.* Once it is clear what is meant by degrees of freedom, it becomes a matter for empirical speculation and research to determine

---

*If, for freedom, distributional considerations take precedence over aggregative ones, if what matters is less how much freedom there is, but how fairly that freedom is distributed, then it could be argued that even in principle such losses could not be offset by gains to holders of productive property (capitalists). Although he does not quite put matters this way, this seems to be Macpherson's position.

whether freedom is well- or ill-served by capitalist market relations. Traditional liberalism, in foreclosing talk of degrees of freedom, effectively precludes investigation of this question. But if we grant—as we should, even from a liberal perspective—that degrees of freedom be taken into account, this question—whether economic liberties promote or detract from freedom—comes to the fore.

And Macpherson's answer—that economic liberties detract from total freedom—is surely very plausible; particularly if, like Macpherson, we deny—in virtue of what we think of human nature—that individuals really conform to the possessive individualist model (the evidence of behavior in capitalist market societies to the contrary). But while Macpherson's view of human nature makes the case against economic liberties more likely, it is not strictly necessary for it. It could be the case, after all, that capitalism, by generating vastly unequal distributions of benefits and burdens, does diminish in aggregate the abilities of people to do what they want.

So long as we abide by the characteristic abstractness of liberal theory, those who insist on the unity of political and economic liberties have an invincible case. But once that abstractness is relaxed—once we admit considerations of institutional impediments and advantages, and of exploitation—the exclusion of economic liberties becomes entirely likely. To this extent, liberal democracy's core theory can be disengaged, as it were, from its market heritage. Does it follow, then, that liberal democratic theory can be revised along the lines Macpherson suggests? A "non-market theory of democracy," as Macpherson would have it, is surely possible. But will it, as Macpherson wants, retain continuity with liberal democracy's theory and practice?

The question of continuity with liberal democracy's core theory can be answered either affirmatively or negatively, depending on how narrowly we construe the core. We have seen that the kind of democratic theory Macpherson advocates can retain the core notion of freedom, and indeed must break with market assumptions, if it can be shown, as seems likely for many concrete historical circumstances, that (in the appropriate sense of "freedom") economic liberties diminish total freedom. However, in advancing a different view of human nature from that of the dominant tradition, Macpherson does substantially modify the core theory's view of interest. By Macpherson's account, individuals cease to be consumers of utilities and become instead developers of powers. They are still maximizers, of course, and the Hobbesian notion of rational agency is retained. The difference lies just in what individuals are thought to maximize—utilities for traditional liberals, powers for Macpherson. If fidelity to the core theory means retention of the core theory's notions of freedom and interest, then Macpherson succeeds on one count and fails on the other. But if the point is just to retain fidelity to the tradition's view of freedom, as seems to be Macpherson's intent, then, it seems, continuity with the dominant tradition is achieved.

But this is a very pale and tenuous continuity. Gone of course is liberal democracy's characteristic abstractness. Gone too is any tendential commitment to a minimal state, at least, if, as seems indisputable, substantial state interference is necessary for insuring equal access to the means of labor and life. And to the extent that Macpherson's view of human nature draws him closer to classical and idealist views of man as a political animal, gone as well is that subordination of the political to the social that is definitive of liberal thought (see chapter 1). Indeed, all that remains is a commitment to political liberty in the sense developed within the dominant tradition—conceived in line with Hobbes' view of freedom and rational agency.

Thus Macpherson's vision of proper political arrangement bears only the most narrow of links with that of the dominant tradition. Yet he is intent in insisting on continuity. So tenuous and slight is the actual continuity, that it is plainly more a political than a theoretical judgment to declare the one continuous with the other. Insisting on continuity is, in essence, a declaration of affiliation with the political *practice* of Western liberal democracies, and not particularly with their theory. Put differently: Macpherson's view of where we should be differs substantially—even radically—from where we are and from where standard liberal democratic theory holds we should be. But his view of how to get from here to there is entirely continuous with liberal democratic political practice. There is no question of a revolutionary break, but instead, of utilizing liberal democratic means—the institutions and procedures of existing liberal democratic polities. The reformed theory Macpherson proposes is a theoretical expression, as it were, of a reformist practice. Macpherson's is a conservative, not a revolutionary, "supercession" of liberal democratic theory. He would go "beyond liberal democracy," but in order to "retrieve" what is valuable in the tradition.

Retrieval

The project of retrieval is, above all, an effort to preserve political continuity, continuity with the dominant political practice of Western, liberal democratic polities. I think it fair to hold that this political affiliation motivates and, to some extent at least, even shapes the character of Macpherson's prescriptions for democratic theory.

There is a passage in "The Maximization of Democracy" where this political motivation becomes virtually explicit. The West, Macpherson writes, must "compete" morally—"in the quality of life it makes possible for its citizens . . . measured in terms of the maximization of each person's powers . . . "[16] But compete for what and with whom? For Isaiah Berlin, the fear of "totalitarianism" implicit, in his view, in commitments to positive liberty has, as with so many recent liberal writers, a distinctly Cold War tinge. Negative liberty is an important part of what the West seeks to retain in its struggle with the East, and it is also a weapon in that struggle. But Macpherson is no Cold Warrior. Indeed, in the very passage where the call for moral competition is issued, Macpherson asserts that both West and East, to the benefit of each, are becoming increasingly alike, to the point that prolonged struggle, or even peaceful competition, *between* them is becoming increasingly nugatory. Neither, by Macpherson's express declaration, is the competition in question *for* the allegiance of the Third World. "Both West and East," Macpherson writes, "are so confident of their technical and cultural superiority to the third world that their behavior is unlikely to be determined by the notion of competing for its favor" (p.22). On the contrary,

> The question, for whose favor are West and East competing, is wrongly posed. The competition is not between West and East for the favor of any third party: *it is between the leaders, the holders of political power, in both East and West, for the support of their own people.* I do not mean that Western voters are likely suddenly to switch to communism, or the communist nations to liberal democracy . . . What is more probable is that the people in the West will demand a levelling up, that is to say, an end to the transfer of powers, and the people in the East, a levelling up in civil and political liberties. Both are becoming technically possible . . . And unless the leaders in the West are prepared to make or accept the fundamental change in the liberal-democratic justifying theory which is now possible, the West stands to lose. (p.22; emphasis added)

What is striking in this passage is not only its optimism (in view of the political history of both the East and West in the years since it was written), but also its conservatism about political institutions. It is the leaders, those who preside over these institutions, who stand to lose; and who must "make or accept fundamental changes" in order to maintain these institutions and their leadership.

Macpherson is never entirely clear who these leaders are. In all likelihood, however, he does not intend just those who actually govern, but rather all those who constitute a society's political and social elite. For Marxists, these "leaders" of liberal democracies can only be capitalists; it would be natural for Marxists to draw the conclusion that the spectre haunting Macpherson's politics is the very spectre that, historically, haunted the thought of so many early liberals and, in a different historical context, continues to haunt the thought of so many of our contemporaries (such as Isaiah Berlin): the spectre of communism. It would not be fair, however, to read Macpherson from the perspective of *The*

Communist Manifesto. For Macpherson plainly does not accept its account of the fundamental, constitutive role of class struggle, nor its view of the state as the orgainzed domination of one class by another. Macpherson is a socialist, but he does not see the world as Marxists do.

Macpherson's socialism is reformist and evolutionary. Unlike most Marxists, he bases a great deal on the achievements of liberal democracy in promoting civil and political liberties. These achievements, he seems to think, are too substantial to jeopardize by attempting any radical transformation of the existing order. The attempt at conceptual retrieval is motivated by this view: Macpherson would refrain from tampering with what is assuredly good enough, and with what is threatened, paradoxically, by those very capitalist market relations with which liberal democracy, since its inception, has been so deeply associated. More orthodox liberals have always thought that "the victory of the West" meant the victory of capitalism. Macpherson categorically rejects this conclusion. For him, the development of productive capacities (under capitalism) creates, at once, the necessity for overcoming capitalism and also the possibility for doing so. "The victory of the West," whatever the overwhelming majority of liberal democrats may tell us, requires socialism.

Whatever we conclude, finally, about the viability of Macpherson's positive positions in political philosophy, their political orientation can now be identified unmistakably. What Macpherson provides is a sustained, theoretical expression of social democracy, not only in the sense already defined (idiosyncratically in the Introduction), but also in the accepted historical sense, of a political movement, rooted in the working class, that began as an attempt to replace capitalism and has become, in country after country, an effort to reform and manage it. Social democracy, in each of its senses, is the left wing of liberalism, of the dominant political practice. It rests its faith on the development of productive capacities and the progressive and continuous evolution of political forms. The established order is conserved, not as most conservatives would have it, by the joyous or even grudging acceptance of market society and possessive individualism, but by the implementation of reforms designed to mitigate the worst features of the existing order and by the development of justifying theories that, while eliminating possessive individualist assumptions, nonetheless retain continuity with the dominant tradition of liberal democratic thought.

There is good reason, I think, to question the claim for theoretical continuity. Macpherson's view of proper political arrangements is too distant from that of more traditional liberal democrats, even though he does aim to sever economic from political liberties while remaining faithful to the liberal democratic (and Hobbesian) view of freedom. What is not in question is the express political continuity with liberal democracy. But this politics is plainly problematic, given Macphersons's substantive normative theory. It is far from clear whether, by a liberal democratic route, we can get from where we are to where Macpherson (and other socialists, including those who affirm expressly revolutionary positions) would like us to be. This fundamental question of socialist politics cannot be settled here. It is enough to note where Macpherson stands, and how his stand affects his theoretical commitment to retrieve, rather than to break from, the dominant tradition.

Where Matters Stand

Those of us who are less sanguine about the existing order, who are aware of the conceptual problems its justifying theory faces, and who realize the distance that must separate a "non-market theory of democracy" from traditional liberal democratic theory, may be less determined than Macpherson to insist on continuity with the dominant tradition in theory and much more wary about respecting the dominant tradition in practice. For us, what is called for is not a different and more satisfactory liberal democratic theory, a social democratic theory (in either of the related senses in contention), but a different kind of theory altogether.

Unfortunately, as noted at the outset, the alternative is not at hand. I would hazard that idealism is not the answer, though it does seem, as has been noted in passing, that this subordinate tradition has generally surpassed the dominant tradition in insight and political sensibility. The most likely direction for research in political theory, I continue to believe, is that pioneered by Marx and later elaborated by Lenin (in *The State and Revolution*, particularly) and others.[17] However, to date, despite all the attention Marxists have lavished on related issues, including the (descriptive) theory of the state, a properly Marxist *political theory* of a sort that could be counterposed to liberal democratic theory or to idealism remains virtually undeveloped and even largely uncharted. It is therefore more a hope than an expectation to find relief from that quarter. Nearly a century and a half of liberal democratic dominance has left us all the poorer politically—to the point where it is far from clear today even what a satisfactory political theory and practice would be like. One point, however, can be suggested, in consequence both of reflecting on Macpherson's example and also in the hope that the direction staked out by Marx and Lenin will at last prove fruitful: that a condition for a satisfactory political theory is a shift in politics or, more exactly, a shift in partisanship in political theory—from the side of the leaders to the side of those who, until now, have been led.

Conclusion

LIBERAL democratic theory has been faulted here on three principal counts. It has been argued that its presupposed notions of freedom and interest, and ultimately its account of rational agency, are historically peculiar and conceptually problematic, even if some of the more blatantly inadequate positions historically associated with the theory in its classical form can be excised. It has been maintained, further, that the very project of combining liberal and democratic judgments on political institutions into a single justifying theory is very likely doomed and, in any case, has not yet successfully been achieved. And it has been suggested that a condition for undertaking such a project—in particular, for maintaining the integrity of the liberal component—is a certain, characteristic abstractness that renders liberal democratic theory inadequate both descriptively (as an account of actual political life) and normatively (as a vision of ideal political arrangements). It is doubtful, moreover, whether this abstractness can be overcome without breaking from liberal democratic theory (except in the most tenuous of senses). These charges, singly and together, amount to a substantial critique of the dominant political theory; and thus to the justifying theory of prevailing political practice.

Liberal democratic political practice *per se* has figured in this discussion—mainly in chapters 8 and 10—only insofar as is necessary to account for liberal democracy's theory. For, strictly speaking, it is liberal democratic theory—not practice—that is in question here. This is why I have hardly even noted liberal democracy's most readily apparent shortcomings: its failure to develop cohesive political communities and a satisfactory style of political participation, the tendency of its characteristic institutions to support and even exacerbate social inequality, social divisions and civil strife, and, worst of all, the substantial contribution liberal democratic states continue to make to irreversible environmental degradation, international injustice and animosity, and the threat of annihilating war. These are very grave failings, to be sure; and are more pressing, plainly, than any of the charges discussed in these pages. But they are not, at least in the first instance, problems with liberal democracy's justifying theory.

Needless to say, it is an awareness of liberal democracy's actual shortcomings, and of the urgency of correcting them, that underlies this critique of liberal democracy's theory. But a critique of liberal democratic theory is, at best, only a first step in coming to terms, critically, with liberal democracy. The connections pertaining between liberal democracy's theory and liberal democratic institutions must be fully and systematically explored. Above all, the vexed question of the relation between liberal democracy and capitalism, a vast and complex issue touched upon above at a number of points, but never explored systematically, remains to be investigated in depth. What I have done here is just a preliminary to that further task. My intent has been only to lay bare what liberal democratic theory is, and to explore a few of its points of vulnerability.

But isn't liberal democracy, however imperfect, nevertheless the best of actually existing forms of political life? And for all its shortcomings, aren't liberal democracy's achievements in promoting civil and political liberties sufficiently impressive to encourage us, like Macpherson, to seek to retain continuity with it, rather than to risk an alternative that, despite all the best intentions, might turn out much worse? And if Marxism is to be that alternative, as seems most plausible, isn't even a quick comparison of existing liberal democratic states with those deemed Marxist enough to make us opt without hesitation for what we already have, even with all its faults? The answers to these questions are, I think, rather less plain than may at first appear.

It need hardly be said that existing communist societies, particularly in their political institutions, are vastly at odds with the spirit and letter of classical Marxian political theory. Whether or not *The Critique of the Gotha Program* or *The State and Revolution* point in the direction of alternative, and more satisfactory, foundations for political life is, of course, very much open to debate. But the experience of those countries deemed communist has, at best, only a very indirect and slight bearing on that debate. It is no exaggeration to claim that, despite the legacy of more than sixty years of purportedly Marxist rule over a vast section of the planet, Marxist politics, at least as regards the governance of post-Revolutionary societies, is even less developed than Marxian political theory.

Still it must be granted that liberal democracies, at least by comparison to communist and other rival political systems, do accord pride of place to civil and political liberties, and even, with due allowance for sometimes astonishing hypocisy, to human rights. Macpherson is surely right to declare that "in the scale of political and civil liberties, the communist nations have no where to go but up." Doubtless, the same judgment applies, perhaps even with greater justice, to the non-communist countries of the Third World. But this pride of place, we know, is precarious. The conceptual devices used to express and defend civil and political liberties—and human rights—are woefully problematic. Thus rights are introduced without adequate theoretical grounding, as a corrective to tendencies deeply inscribed in the core theory, tendencies that threaten to undo not only civil and political liberties, but even the most fundamental sense of human dignity or worth. And the liberal component itself retains its integrity and function only at grave theoretical costs. Civil and political liberties, then, are not nearly so secure in liberal democratic theory as may at first appear. And, as is all too evident, neither are they any more secure in the day-by-day functioning of liberal democratic polities. The problem is not just that liberal democracies fall short of their theoretical pretensions. Very likely, any political arrangement would. Rather, liberal democracy has not succeeded, in either theory or practice, in providing adequate bases for maintaining what its defenders, and also its non-revolutionary critics, seek to "retrieve." That liberal democracy does aim to accord pride of place to what it construes as civil and political liberties—and to human rights—is undeniably to its credit. But it does not, and I think we can now say, cannot succeed in the attempt. It was argued in chapter 8 that, appearance to the contrary, liberal democracy is not in fact true to its democratic commitments. It might now be added, in light of the discussion just concluded, that it does not measure up very well either to what is attractive in the liberal component.

I have argued that, in all likelihood, it is vain to attempt to correct these shortcomings while continuing to do politics and political theory, however critically, within the dominant tradition. Neither adding a theory of justice to liberal democratic theory nor expunging "possessive individualist" elements from the inherited theory will suffice to produce a genuine and satisfactory "supercession" of liberal democracy. We should not hesitate, then, despite what is meritorious in the dominant tradition, to abandon the attempt at continuity. This is, we have seen, more a political than a theoretical choice. I think it desirable, even urgent, that we choose against the old politics. Liberal democracy's defense of civil and political liberties, and its commitment to human rights, should be paralleled, as it were, rather than incorporated, in a theory and practice discontinuous with the dominant, but defective and perilous, tradition.

We do not have that alternative at hand. And it is with more hope than reasoned conviction that I have speculated here where it might be fruitfully sought. Still it is urgent that we look.

Notes

Introduction

1. John Rawls, *A Theory of Justice* (Cambridge, Mass.: Harvard University Press, 1971), p.2

Chapter One. An Overview of Liberal Democratic Theory

1. John Locke's political writings, though antedating Mill's by more than a century, might count as an exception. Locke is certainly a liberal, at least with respect to individuals' control over property and its disposition and, arguably also, on questions of religious liberty and freedom of thought. Moreover, Locke's major political work, *The Second Treatise on Civil Government*, provides an elaborate defense of majority rule voting, the characteristic collective decision procedure of democrats. Nonetheless, by substantially restricting the extent of the franchise, and by removing most questions of social policy from collective control, Locke cannot count as a *democrat* in the requisite sense. It is best, then, to regard Locke as an important precursor, but not quite an exponent, of liberal democratic theory.

2. On the decline of a proper sense of *the political* under the dominance of liberal thought, see Sheldon S. Wolin, *Politics and Vision; Continuity and Innovation in Western Political Thought* (Boston: Little Brown, 1960), ch. 9.

3. Max Weber, "Politics as a Vocation," in eds., *From Max Weber: Essays in Sociology*, H.H. Gerth and C. Wright Mills, eds., (New York: Oxford University Press, 1958), p. 78. Weber's celebrated definition of the state as "a human community that (successfully) claims the monopoly of the legitimate use of physical force within a given territory" articulates what has long been agreed upon in Western political thought, at least since Bodin and Macchiavelli—that is, since the emergence of the nation state itself.

4. See Robert Nozick's *Anarchy, State and Utopia* (New York: Basic Books, 1974) and Ronald Dworkin, *Taking Rights Seriously* (Cambridge, Harvard Press, 1977).

5. David Hume, *A Treatise of Human Nature*, Bk. II, part 3, sec. 3; and *An Enquiry Concerning the Principles of Morals*, sec. 1.

6. Jeremy Bentham, *Handbook of Political Fallacies*, H.A. Larrabee, ed., (Baltimore, Johns Hopkins Press, 1952), p. 213

7. See David Gauthier, "Reason and Maximization," *Canadian Journal of Philosophy* (March 1975), vol. iv, no. 3, esp. pp. 413-15.

8. See my *The Politics of Autonomy: A Kantian Reading of Rousseau's Social Contract* (Amherst: University of Massachusetts Press, 1976), pp. 59-62.

Chapter Two. Freedom

1. An indispensible point of departure for any serious investigation of unfreedom (in the liberal sense) is chapter 4 of Felix Oppenheim's *Dimensions of Freedom* (New York: St. Martin, 1961)

2. See Robert Nozick, "Coercion" in Morgenbesser, Suppes, and White, eds., *Philosophy, Science, and Method: Essays in Honor of Ernest Nagel* (New York: St. Martin, 1969).

3. This point is argued by Isaiah Berlin in the Introduction to *Four Essays on Liberty* (Oxford: Oxford University Press, 1969), esp. pp. liii-lviii; and also in "Two Concepts of Liberty," *ibid.*, pp. 122-124.

4. Kant, *The Foundations of the Metaphysics of Morals*, 2nd section, esp. pp. 414-411. Kant's express formulation is as follows: "whoever wills the end wills also (necessarily according to reason) the only means to it which are in his power" (418).

5. See David Gauthier, "Reason and Maximization," *Canadian Journal of Philosophy* (March 1975), 4(3): 413-15.

6. Mill, *On Liberty*, chap. 3.

7. *Ibid.*, ch. 4.

Chapter Three. Interests

1. This way of construing the problem of collective choice originates in the classic formulations of Kenneth Arrow; see his *Social Choice and Individual Values* (2nd ed.; New York: Wiley, 1951, 1963).

2. See Kenneth Arrow, "Public and Private Values" in Sidney Hook, ed. *Human Values and Economic Pollicy* (New York: New York University Press, 1967), pp. 15-17.

3. See Amartya K. Sen, *Collective Choice and Social Welfare* (San Francisco: Holden Day, 1970). ch. 10, sec. 2, and R. Niemi and H. Weisberg, "A Mathematical Solution for the Probability of the Paradox of Voting," *Behavioral Sciences* (1968) vol. 13. Between 10 and 15 alternatives, the probability of a cyclical majority

surpasses 50 percent. By 20 alternatives, the probability is approximately .68. By 45 alternatives, it is nearly .83.

4. This line of investigation was pioneered by Duncan Black, *The Theory of Committees and Elections* (New York: Cambridge, 1948), and Arrow, *Social Choice and Individual Values*, ch. 7, and has advanced considerably, at least on the formal side, in recent years. See K. Inada, "The Simple Majority Decision Rule," *Econometrica* (July 1969), 37(3): 490-506; and Sen, chs. 10 and 10*.

5. This result was first demonstrated by Black, *Theory of Committees and Elections*.

6. It has been known for some time that this condition can be reformulated so as to admit cardinal measurements of welfare, without sacrificing its intuitive appeal or its role in formulating the problem of social choice. See Jerome Rothenberg, *The Measurement of Social Welfare* (Englewood Cliffs, N.J.: Prentice-Hall, 1961), ch. 6, esp. pp. 132-45.

7. *An Introduction to the Principles of Morals and Legislation* (New York: Hafner, 1948), p.3.

8. Robert Paul Wolff, Jr., "Beyond Tolerance," in Wolff, Herbert Marcuse, and Barrington Moore, Jr., *A Critique of Pure Tolerance* (Boston: Beacon, 1965).

9. Brian Barry, *Political Argument*, (London: Routledge & Keagan Paul, 1965) ch.10.

10. Sir George Cornewall Lewis, "Remarks on the Use and Abuse of Some Political Terms" (London, 1832); cited in op. cit., pp. 190-91.

11. For a discussion of this problem in a different context (with reference to Rousseau's idealist defense of majority rule voting), see my *The Politics of Autonomy: A Kantian Reading of Rousseau's Social Contract* (Amherst: University of Massachusetts Press, 1976), pp. 88-95.

Chapter Four. Rational Agency

1. See David Gauthier, "Reason and Maximization," *Canadian Journal of Philosophy* (March 1975), 4(3): 411-33. Among cases where the outcomes of individuals' choices do *not* depend upon the choices of others, are those where the outcomes of alternative choices are known, and those where choices are made under conditions of uncertainty. Each has been subjected to extensive investigation in the literature on rational choice; however, these cases will be largely ignored here. The context of interdependent action is analyzed in the mathematical theory of games.

2. See Gauthier, "Reason and Maximization," for a sustained attempt to develop such an account that is particularly lucid in calling attention to the problems in the way of constructing a fully adequate theory.

3. Karl Marx, Frederick Engels, *Collected Works*, vol. 3 (New York: Lawrence

and Wishart, 1975), esp. pp. 270-82 and 306-21. In Marx's view, extrinsic relations pertain between workers, as well as between workers and capitalists.

    4. Hegel, *The Phenomenology of Mind*, B, IV, A, "Independence and Dependence of Self-Consciousness: Lordship and Bondage."

    5. C. B. Macpherson, *The Political Theory of Possessive Individualism* (Oxford: Oxford University Press, 1962).

Chapter Five. The Liberal Democratic Project

    1. Amartya K. Sen, "The Impossibility of a Paretian Liberal," *Journal of Political Economy*, (1970), 77: 152-57; and *Collective Choice and Social Welfare* (San Francisco: Holden Day, 1970), ch. 6.

    2. C. B. Macpherson, *The Life and Times of Liberal Democracy* (Oxford: Oxford University Press, 1977). See especially chapter 1.

Chapter Six. Private and Public

    1. John Stuart Mill, *On Liberty*, David Spitz, ed. (New York: Norton, 1975), p. 12.

    2. See Joel Feinberg, *Social Philosophy* (Englewood Cliffs, N.J.: Prentice Hall, 1973), ch. 2.

    3. For a sustained reading of *On Liberty* along these lines, see Robert Paul Wolff, *The Poverty of Liberalism* (Boston: Beacon Press, 1968). ch. 1.

    4. Mill, *On Liberty*, pp. 10-11.

    5. J. C. Rees, "A Re-reading of Mill on Liberty," *Political Studies* (1960), 7 (2): 113-29.

    6. Among those who have taken discussion of this topic furthest, see Richard Wollheim, "John Stuart Mill and the Limits of State Action," *Social Research* (Spring 1973), 40(1): 1-30; and C. L. Ten, "Mill on Self-Regarding Actions," *Philosophy* (1968), no. 43. Both Ten and Wollheim effectively distance themselves from that tendency among interpreters of Mill who speak of "interests" as the objects of harm, but this difference is of no account here. Both contend that what Mill seeks to protect from interference are actions not affecting (and therefore not harming) others or affecting them only by producing psychic discomfort as a result of the distaste that others have for the action. Thus for Ten, only *directly* affecting others counts, where "according to Mill an action indirectly affects others, or what amounts to the same thing, the interests of others, if it affects their happiness simply because they dislike it, or find it repugnant or immoral." For Wollheim, Mill's class of self-regarding actions "consists of those actions which either have no effects upon others or, if they do have an effect, have this only via certain beliefs these other hold." This is not the place to quarrel over textual interpreta-

Notes   211

tions, but I would hazard that both Ten and Wollheim are better seen as *correcting*, rather than *interpreting*, Mill. In any case, neither Ten's nor Wollheim's account escapes the kind of damaging relativism that, I argue, undoes Mill's efforts at marking off the private sphere. In each case, what counts as harm *is* relative to the norms and practices of society. Thus for both writers, and of course also for Mill, you harm me if you destroy my property—but that property is mine only in virtue of institutional arrangements and practices of the sort the liberal principle is supposed to evaluate.

7. This list is taken from Feinberg, *Social Philosophy*, p. 26, and is characteristic, though hardly exhaustive, of the kinds of interests legal writers invoke.

8. The most celebrated and politically influential version of such a theory of interest is, of course, Rousseau's account of the *general will* as the (rational) will of each person *qua* citizen. See my *The Politics of Autonomy: A Kantian Reading of Rousseau's Social Contract* (Amherst: University of Massachusetts Press, 1976), part 1.

9. See Robert Paul Wolff, *The Poverty of Liberalism*, pp. 23-25.

Chapter Seven. Rights

1. John Locke, *The Second Treatise of Government*, esp. chs. 2 & 3.

2. Locke, *Second Treatise of Government*, ch. 9.

3. See Maurice Cranston, *What Are Human Rights?* (London: Tapliker, 1973), p. 1.

4. See Martin Golding. "Towards a Theory of Human Rights, *The Monist*, vol. 52, no. 4 (October 1968), pp. 521-49.

5. It has been argued that, historically, liberals have fallen into either of two camps, precisely over the question of whether or not they take rights "seriously." See Ronald Dworkin, *Taking Rights Seriously* (Cambridge, Mass.: Harvard University Press, 1977j, ch. 1. Roughly, the split is between those who are, in their underlying moral philosophies, utilitarians, and those who are not. In this regard, see also H. L. A. Hart, "Between Utility and Rights," in Alan Ryan, ed., *The Idea of Freedom: Essays in Honour of Isaiah Berlin* (Oxford: Oxford University Press, 1979).

6. S. I. Benn, "Rights," *The Encyclopedia of Philosophy* (New York: Collier MacMillan, 1967) 195-99.

7. The best known of these critiques is of course Marx's in his early writings, see *The Economic and Philosophic Manuscripts* (1844), especially the final section of the first Manuscript. I have argued elsewhere that, for the early Marx, alienated labor is an "inversion" of the ideal Kantian order in which persons have "dignity." (*Würde*), while things merely have (exchange) value *(Preis)*. See my "Alienation as Heteronomy," *The Philosophical Forum* (2-4): pp. 256-68.

8. This conservative lament is echoed in Joseph Schumpeter's speculations

on the likelihood of capitalism's demise. Schumpeter did not look forward to the passing of capitalism, but he considered the prospects of a fully commercial society to be grim indeed. See *Capitalism, Socialism, and Democracy* (New York: Harper and Row, 1942), part 2.

9. See James Tobin, "On Limiting the Domain of Inequality," *Journal of Law and Economics* (October 1970), 13:269, and Arthur Okun, *Equality and Efficiency: The Big Trade Off* (Washington: Brookings, 1975), p. 9.

10. See Robert Nozick, *Anarchy, State, and Utopia* (New York: Bask Books, 1974). The starting-point for this extended and intricately argued neo-Lockean tract is the assertion, declared at the very outset, that "individuals have rights, and there are things no person or group may do to them (without violating their rights)." Nozick never tells us what the source of these rights is, or on what basis they are ascribed.

Chapter Eight. Representation

1. Rousseau, *The Social Contract*, book III, ch. 15.

2. It should be noted, however, that for Rousseau, an idealist with a quite different notion of interest from that which liberal democrats suppose, the point of aggregation is not, as for liberal democrats, to achieve the optimal level of social welfare, given individuals' interests, but rather to discover what "the general interest," the true interest of each individual qua citizen is. See my *The Politics of Autonomy: A Kantian Reading of Rousseau's Social Contract* (Amherst: University of Massachusetts Press, 1976), pp. 59-71.

Chapter Nine. Freedom and Exploitation

1. Among the best known are F. A. Hayek, *The Constitution of Liberty* (Chicago: University of Chicago Press, 1960) and Milton Friedman, *Capitalism and Freedom* (Chicago: University of Chicago Press, 1962).

2. See Thomas Scanlon, "Liberty, Contract and Contribution," in Gerald Dworkin, Gordon Bermant, and Peter G. Brown, eds., *Markets and Morals* (Washington, D.C.: Halsted Press, 1977), pp. 43-65. In chapter 8, we saw how markets might also be defended on aggregative grounds, for promoting social welfare. Scanlon points to yet other considerations supporting markets. Thus the market mechanism could be defended for explicitly distributional reasons. The argument might run as follows: given any initial distributor of goods taken to be just, if two parties would prefer the result of a bilateral exchange, surely it would be just to allow the exchange to take place, and unjust to prevent it. Traditionally, libertarian defenders of markets have been more inclined to speak of freedom than of justice, as one would expect of proper liberal democrats. But with the currency of talk of

justice today, following in the wake of Rawls' influential A Theory of Justice, it is not surprising to find clever defenders of markets shifting ground in order to defend market arrangements, in roughly the way just indicated, by appeal to justice. See, for example, Robert Nozick, Anarchy, State, Utopia (New York: Basic Books, 1974).

3. This line of analysis is suggested by G. A. Cohen, "Capitalism, Freedom, and the Proletariat," in Alan Ryan ed., The Idea of Freedom: Essays in Honour of Isaiah Berlin (Oxford: Oxford University Press, 1979) and especially in "Capitalism, Socialism and Freedom" (unpublished typescript). See also Charles Taylor, "What's Wrong with Negative Liberty," also in Ryan.

Chapter Ten. Beyond Liberal Democracy?

1. See the Introduction. The expression is John Rawls'. See A theory of Justice (Cambridge, Mass.: Hartford University Press, 1971), p. 3. Empahsis mine.

2. See especially Macpherson, Democratic Theory: Essays in Retrieval (Oxford: Oxford University Press, 1973). Also pertinent, though more for the critique of the dominant tradition than for its reconstitution are The Political Theory of Possessive Individualism: Hobbes to Locke (Oxford: Oxford University Press, 1962), The Real World of Democracy (Oxford: Oxford University Press, 1966), and The Life and Times of Liberal Democracy (Oxford: Oxford University Press, 1977).

3. See Macpherson, "The Maximization of Democracy," in Democratic Theory, pp. 19-23.

4. Ibid., pp. 95-119.

5. See Isaiah Berlin, Four Essays on Liberty (Oxford: Oxford University Press, 1969), pp. 118-72.

6. Macpherson, Democratic Theory, p. 95.

7. By "human power" is meant "a man's ability to use and develop his capacities." See esp. ibid., pp. 41-42. The concept is, of course, taken from Hobbes.

8. Ibid., p. 98.

9. Ibid., p. 104.

10. Ibid.

11. Ibid., p. 42.

12. See Rousseau, The Social Contract, book II, ch. eleven. For further discussion, see my The Politics of Autonomy: A Kantian Reading of Rousseau's Social Contract (Amherst: University of Mass. Press, 1976), pp. 187-92.

13. Macpherson, Democratic Theory, p. 108.

14. I think Macpherson does indeed capture a strain of classical liberal theory that Berlin and other contemporary liberal writers tend to overlook. Mill, for example, defended liberty, at least in part, on grounds that it develops a critical, idiosyncratic character type that is conducive to the development of individuals'

capacities. In "Problems of a Non-Market Theory of Democracy," *Democratic Theory*, pp. 39-76, Macpherson contributes substantially to the precision of this claim.

15. A similar argument can be gotten out of Mill. See his *On Liberty*, ch. 3.

16. Macpherson, *Democratic Theory*, p. 20.

17. For an elaboration and expansion of some of Lenin's positions, see Etienne Balibar, *On the Dictatorship of the Proletariat* (London: New Left Books, 1977). Also see my "Balibar on the Dictatorship of the Proletariat," *Politics and Society* (1977), 7(1): 69-84.

Conclusion

1. See C. B. Macpherson, *Democratic Theory: Essays in Retrieval* (Oxford: Oxford University Press, 1973), p. 22.

Index